TEACHING YOUR WINGS TO FLY

TEACHING YOUR

WINGS TO FLY

The Nonspecialist's Guide to Movement Activities for Young Children

Anne Lief Barlin

with Ruthe Gluckson and Mady Taylor

Photographs by Hella Hammid
Music Consultant, Mady Taylor

Learning Through Movement

Acknowledgments

I will forever be grateful for the editing, coordinating, and hand holding by Ruthe Gluckson and Mady Taylor. My thanks to Trudi Schoop and Miriam Sherman for reading and helping with portions of the manuscript. Thanks to Kay Tabada and her first and second graders at Carthay Center School in Los Angeles.

To my grandson, Ely Ben Mennin

Library of Congress Cataloging in Publication Data

Barlin, Anne Lief.
   Teaching your wings to fly.

   Includes index.
   1. Dancing—Children's dances—Study and teaching.
2. Movement—Aesthetics of.   I. Gluckson, Ruthe, joint
author.   II. Taylor, Mady, joint author.   III. Title.
GV1799.B318   793.3   77-20894
ISBN 0-87620-892-8

Library of Congress Catalog Card Number: 77-20894
ISBN: 0-87620-892-8
Y-8928-7

Current Printing (last number):
10 9 8 7 6 5 4 3 2

Art Direction: Vinje + Reid Design Studio

Printed in the United States of America

Learning Through Movement
2728 N.C.R. 25E
Bellvue, Colorado 80512

Contents

From Structure to Freedom

A small child needs the security
Of a structure; a boundary
A cradle; a crib
A home
Within which s/he can
    freely s—t—r—e—t—c—h.

S/he grows, feeling the strength
Feeling the growing strength
Deep Down
In the core of the body.

Loving adults become aware that
S/he is growing and secure
And trusting.
We carefully, gently,
Expand the boundaries.
The child reaches out....
We open them wider....
S/he stretches muscles
        will
        imagination
        brain
        SELF

The trust deepens. The confidence grows.
S/he reaches farther
And touches others.
Strengths are multiplied.
More confidence
To explore; to experiment
To take chances!
To create an ever-widening
Glorious
Joyous
LARGE WORLD

Just a reflection of that good feeling
Deep down
In the core of the body.

How to Use the Book and Plan Your Lessons

This book is specifically designed for you, the classroom teacher of young children. Teachers frequently ask, "How do I start? What's the first thing I do? Is there a sequence I can follow?"

Dance movement, because it is an art form, cannot be learned in a linear, sequential pattern. I see the dance-movement experience as a huge spiral, something like the indoor high-rise parking lots in big cities. You begin on the ground floor and spiral your way up to the next level.

The book is arranged so that each of the ten parts in "The Movement Activities" represents a different area of the dance-movement experience. Each of these areas begins on the "ground floor." On the next level, you will find the same area represented, but with the greater sophistication required by Development I. On the next level you find Development II, and so on. The children learn and grow in all of the areas simultaneously before moving up to a new level. Here is how to use the book.

Choose the *first* movement activity in *any* of the ten parts. Find something that is appealing to you and that you will feel comfortable with. At the beginning of each activity you will see its goals and the age level for which it is intended. Be flexible. Often a movement can be adapted for other age levels with a slight change of motivation. When you see (A) after the ages listed for a movement, that movement can be used for older children if you adapt the motivation. Stay with the beginning exercises and be sure to cover each of the ten parts before going on to the Developments.

Arrange your lesson plans so that you include the *beginnings* of as many areas as possible. (It's all right to repeat the children's favorites, but when you feel that they are ready to go ahead or when there is a new area that you want them to experience, move on.)

Remember that the goal expressed at the beginning of each exercise may be a year away. Every child, every group, and every teacher works at a different pace. The particular dynamics between teacher and child and between teacher and group vary greatly.

Each movement activity is written in the sequence that I have found to be most effective in presenting the material. You will notice that some exercises begin with "Teacher to Students." In these cases, instructions and motivation are immediately clear to you and your students. Other exercises begin with "To the Teacher," because it will help you to have some preparation before communicating with the students.

When it seemed crucial, the text states how many repetitions are desirable. In other cases, watch for fatigue or restlessness.

Prepare yourself to teach the movement activities that have accompaniments by listening carefully to the music before you go to class. Clap the rhythm of the movement or beat it out on a drum, so you become completely familiar and comfortable with it. The enclosed records contain ethnic music. They have locked bands—when the needle reaches the end of a band it rests in the area between bands, instead of moving into the next band. This means that when the music stops you can remain with your class and end the activity gracefully, instead of being obliged to rush off to lift the needle before the next band begins. Feel free to explore and experiment with many kinds of music. You can find a wide selection of classical, jazz, rock, and electronic music recordings in the catalog compiled by the Children's Book and Music Center of Los Angeles.

Remember as you choose your activities for each lesson that a really good lesson plan has a design. It's conceived with a beginning, a middle, and an end; like a work of art, it has a feeling of flow. Although the specifics may not be completely planned out ahead of time, here is a general outline for each lesson.

Introduction. I like starting a class with a ritual. For instance, if the children are very young and the class is small enough, we sit on the floor close together. We talk with each other on a personal level. If the class is too large for this intimacy, I start with a familiar warm-up exercise, or a rhythmic game. In any case, it is important that the children feel unthreatened when they first enter the movement class.

Second Section. When the group is functioning comfortably and accepting the environment as a place for work and fun, I challenge them with body techniques. We do these early in the lesson because they require a great deal of energy.

Third Section. This section is relatively quiet. The children need a change of pace and a change of place. I may do an "Invisible Strings" exercise; an improvisation based on a story, such as "Birds in the Nest" from "Group Sways"; or an exercise in emotional expression, such as "Moving Colors." Or the class may become an audience for children who have been working on original material.

Fourth Section. In this section I do a variety of progressions. In addition to being culmination exercises, most progressions allow great physical and emotional release.

Finale. My favorite ending (and the children's too) for most classes is leaps. Leaps become the dessert at the end of the lesson.

This general lesson plan is based on a class time of about an hour. If you have only a half-hour for your movement session, allow some time for warm-ups at the beginning and progressions at the end. In the middle of the class, include body techniques and creative expression in alternate sessions.

Note to Teachers of English as a Second Language. Teachers of English as a second language find that when children move with words, those words take on real meaning for them. A child who is placing a foot "front and side and back" becomes kinaesthetically aware of what those words mean. Movement activities that are especially valuable to the teacher of English as a second language have "ESL" listed among their goals.

After some twenty years of teaching dance in private studios, in 1965 I began to teach in public schools. I encountered many new problems. I asked myself many questions. When I began to train classroom teachers to use dance movement, many more questions arose.

Gradually I began to formulate my philosophy of teaching. Here then are some of *my* questions and some of *my* answers. I hope they will be helpful to you.

Quotation marks denote words spoken to the children by the teacher. *Three dots*...indicate the passage of time, so students can absorb or respond to what the teacher has said. An asterisk indicates a term explained in the Glossary.

QUESTIONS OR PROBLEMS

The Aesthetic Experience

Question: How can I give the children a truly aesthetic experience?

Answer: It is so important that they learn early that the world is made of far more than the plastic environment in which most of them live. There is beauty in materials that are woven, molded, and carved. There is beauty, nature-designed. It is possible to live with this beauty always, by finding it within ourselves and expressing it in our environment. How can this best be done?

Design exercises which stretch the imagination and use images which evoke aesthetic responses. But more specifically, what *is an aesthetic experience?* When the children are doing ''Tree Shapes,'' they are having an aesthetic experience. Why?

Because they are having a *total* experience. They are involved through their intellects, their bodies, their senses, their emotions, and their imaginations. Let's analyze that.

How are they involved through their intellects? They must hear, understand, and interpret the meaning of my verbal instructions. They must have experience and knowledge of the actual subject.

How are they involved through their bodies? That one is easy. They are obviously moving. But there is a deeper body awareness that you are encouraging here. They are becoming aware of where their bodies are

in space. They are aware of the shapes and designs that their bodies are spontaneously making. You know how exciting that is to you.

How are they involved through their senses? Each child is deeply involved through imagination in the image of being a tree. Let's take one sense at a time. The child hears: the crash of thunder; the crackling of fire; the rustling of branches; the music of the wind. The child tastes: the rain drenching its leaves; the cold, delicate snow. The child smells: the fire; the fresh mountain air; the forest after the rain. The child touches: the wind; the rain; the fire; its own branches (limbs). The child sees: the changing patterns, shapes, and designs made by her/his own body; the partner's body; other groupings nearby. The child's kinaesthetic sense is awakened and alerted. It responds to: the lightning slashes; the downpour of rain; the weight of the snow on its branches. The experience is deepened because the child can feel in her/his muscles what s/he is seeing.

How are the children involved through their emotions? They are being encouraged to express the full range of their emotions: fear, anger, sadness, tenderness, peace, and joy. Here is an opportunity to express these emotions beyond the moderate, normally acceptable level. The children can exert a great deal of energy and express themselves completely.

Why does it trouble me when a teacher asks, "Can we use crepe paper instead of scarves?" or "Can we make drums out of tin cans and rubber?" Sure, if the substitute materials can be made aesthetically beautiful. Most of the time when I have to do without, I prefer to have the children use their imaginations and their bodies. They are always beautiful. The important thing is that I consciously and consistently work toward establishing for the children an environment that develops and expands their level of taste. I must use materials with beautiful textures, shapes, and colors. I must use musical instruments with beautiful tones. I must use aesthetic imagery. And, by no means least important, I must be aware of my own physical appearance and voice quality.

Audience Education

Question: How can I get the children to sit still long enough to watch one another?

Answer: I think the problem is cultural. Most children have little opportunity to learn to take responsibility for being a good audience. Their viewing experience is with television, where they feel free to talk during a performance because they have no live contact with the performer.

I try to create performance situations in the movement sessions in which children can learn to "watch quietly until Jeannie is finished" before they guess what she is. I tell them, "Try not to laugh or boo. You know how bad you feel when someone laughs at you. And you know how good you feel when your friends applaud you."

Children need help in becoming aware that a live performer is affected by the audience's response as strongly as the audience is affected by the performance.

Children also need help in becoming constructive critics (see "Color Dances," page 172). "Show us how *you* would do it; maybe Patty will like and use your suggestion" creates a sharing and giving environment.

3

Back Problems

Question: Is there any way I can help children who have backs that curve inward deeply (lordosis* curve)?

Answer: It is important to understand that there can be many reasons for that curve. Sometimes it is part of the natural body structure. Sometimes it stems from a poor body image. Sometimes it is a result of poor dance or gymnastics training, where flexibility is stressed and strength and alignment are ignored.

To be sure that I am doing the appropriate thing, I must choose body techniques that help develop body alignment *and* strength *and* flexibility for the back. I must *balance* these exercises so I don't concentrate on one and neglect the others.

One way to begin the correction of back problems is with the "Baby Kitten" activity (page 72). Put your hand on the lowest part of the back of the child you want to help and say, "These are the muscles you want to make strong. . . . Pull up your tummy and push hard against my hand." If you can get that child to try the same action in a standing position, you're on the road to success. Be sure to incorporate the "Centers of Light" (page 85) image along with this focus on the back muscles, so that other parts of the body don't fall out of alignment.

The Boy-Girl Problem

Question: How can I handle the boy-girl problem in movement activities that require coordinated movement by two or more people?

Answer: When you say, "Take a partner" and the children automatically stay with their own sex, leave it alone—at first. Be confident that the fulfillment that they get from the movement activity will eventually override their inhibitions. Wait for the moment when they are completely involved and having fun. At that moment say, "Hurry, Mary needs a partner to do the 'Mirror Leap.'" When I know that they have accepted the dance-movement goals and that they now trust me, my attitude can change to "Don't be silly about this. It's spoiling the class. We need a group of three for the next slide, so come on in, Fred, just join Michelle and Anita. You don't have to marry them. All you have to do is slide with them." At this, the children will probably laugh and relax.

When *doing* the slide has become more important to Fred than holding up the group activity, the problem has taken care of itself.

"But It Hurts!"

Question: What shall I do when a child refuses to do a particular exercise because "it hurts"?

Answer: Many children have not learned to accept pain as a normal part of the growing process. They feel that they are not expected to do anything that is not completely comfortable. To those children I say, "Sure, it hurts most of us to do that at first. It hurts because those ligaments or muscles are too tight. They're telling you that they need stretching. It's your body's way of talking to you. We call that a 'good

hurt.' If you keep doing it, you will get more and more stretch and pretty soon it will begin to feel really good to do the movement." You can also say, "Let's play a game. We'll all say 'ouch' together while we stretch." (See "Licorice Candy," page 53.) Children can learn through their bodies that some pains and struggles are worthwhile.

Remember, an exercise is not necessarily good *because* it hurts. Be sure that each exercise is physiologically appropriate for each child.

Competition

Question: How do you feel about competition?

Answer: I find that my value system is contrary to many of the accepted norms. I am constantly asking myself questions like:

Why do we assume that the leader is superior?

Why do we assume that the fastest person is the winner?

Why do we assume that it is best to be first?

Why do we assume that it is "unmanly" to show emotion?

Why do we assume that "good girls" are not aggressive?

Why do we assume that because something is new, it is necessarily better?

Why do we assume that the majority is right?

I would like to expose the children to a humanistic point of view from which they can learn the satisfactions that come with being responsible, cooperative, sensitive, loving human beings. Movements like "Invisible Strings," "Balloon in a Hurricane," and "The Choo-Choo Train" attempt to reverse the conditioning most of us grew up with.

In "Table-Top Waves" and "Giant Rubber Band Hinges" the children find it far more satisfying to "move with the slowest member of the group" than to be an outsider.

In "Passing the Shoe," they learn that taking your time to extend your torso—instead of racing—can make the significant difference between

Correcting A Child

Question: How can I correct a student without embarrassing the child in front of the group?

Answer: It's best, of course, if you can avoid focusing on the individual child. It's rarely necessary. Somehow children always know without being told that they are not doing a movement in harmony with the rest of the class. Their bodies seem to tell them. It's an uncomfortable feeling and it's important to help them. Here are some of the ways I can handle this problem.

While the entire class is continuing an activity, walk over to a particular child and touch and move with her/him.

Suggest a new motivation to the entire class that will create a positive response in that particular child. For the child who is using only one leg for a skip, say to the group, "How many legs do all of you have?... Let's all hold the balloon carefully... touch it with one knee... and hop ... now the other knee... and hop." It seldom hurts those who are already accomplished to repeat a movement successfully while others are catching up.

I can make a point of finding some time alone with the child who needs help. And of course, I must accentuate the positive.

hurting your back or comfortably achieving flexibility. In "The Secret" (a Development of "Invisible Strings"), the boys discover that it is quite fulfilling to express tender feelings. In "Dinosaurs" it is the slowest person who really wins.

Our commercial world bombards us with the erroneous notion that if it's new, it's better. Many of our children internalize this value and say in class, "We've done that before." My answer is, "That's why we're doing it again. Now that we're familiar with it, we can really try to get high up in the air" or "We can concentrate on straightening our knees this time." The truth is that children love repetition. They love hearing the same stories over and over again. They love repeating familiar things that have given them joy.

I remember demonstrating a mirror movement to a large class of fourth-graders. At the end of the demonstration I asked the observers, "How many of you think that the reflection is responsible for the success of this exercise?" Most of them raised their hands. "How many of you think that the initiator is responsible for the success of the exercise?" A few hands lifted tentatively. "We won!" shouted one of the students. "Yes," I said, "you won the vote, but the minority was right." Movement class is a wonderful place to allow the children to question in their own terms existing and changing values.

Discipline

Question: How do I discipline the children when they get wild?

Answer: In general, I teach a "no nonsense" class. My love of dance and the joy of sharing it are uppermost. My love for the children is in constant evidence. Therefore I don't feel guilty about not giving some children license to spoil the experience for the others.

Children sometimes get so stimulated that I lose them. There are many tricks for getting them back to attention, depending on what is happening at the moment. If they have been running all over the room and you want to get them back; if they think they can anticipate the next move and their attention strays; or if you need to spark their interest, to make them alert—try these.

Relocate the class. Gesture to the class and whisper, "Come quickly. I have a secret." It makes little difference what you tell them, although it's fun to test your own imagination at

these moments. In any case, just whispering what is going to happen next will suffice. Or you can ask, "Would you like to hear a story? Let's all sit near the window." Or say, "You did that very well. Let's all sit here and watch while you do it for us one at a time."

Reverse the expected. Say, "Let's do the opposite" or "Let's do it backwards" and see what you and your children come up with.

Change the dynamics. If the movement activity has been slow, requiring deep concentration, change to a fast, vigorous traveling movement.

Change formations. If the class has been moving in unison, suggest: "Half the class watch the other half"; "This time with a partner"; "Find another partner"; or "Everyone sit down front and be an audience."

Ask questions. Involve the children with questions like "What kind of bird has the widest wingspread in the world?" or "Why is a slide called a slide?"

Reason with them (with relevance). "If you're being too noisy, you won't be able to hear the next part of the story."

Have a signal. "Every time I shake the tambourine, you freeze. It means that I want to tell you what will happen next."

Do I Have To Move?

Question: Do I have to move?

Answer: If you are physically handicapped or too stiff (or too old?—never!) to execute a movement that you want your children to experience, you can still inspire and motivate them. Using your voice rhythmically and with feeling, along with simple arm and head gestures, can bring the images to the children and motivate them to move.

Do The Opposite

Question: There are many days when I just don't feel "creative." It makes me feel a little guilty, but should I borrow someone else's ideas?

Answer: Sure, it's a good way to start. In time, the children usually open me up with their natural creativity. Once, in the middle of class, I accidentally discovered a device for breaking through to my own creativity. I stopped in the middle of a movement and said, "Let's do the opposite." It worked like magic!

It's surprising how many things can be reversed—and how much fun that can be! A movement that has always traveled forward can be done backwards; a movement that has always been done in place can be made to travel; something always done to music can be done in silence. "Let's do the opposite" makes old patterns break down and imaginations flow. It's an open sesame to creativity.

Glasses

Question: A student protests, "Why did you ask me to take off my glasses? I'm supposed to wear them all the time. I can't see you without my glasses."

Answer: I encourage everyone to try to get along without glasses during movement sessions. It becomes a further challenge to the development of the kinaesthetic sense and body awareness. Removing their glasses also forces students to use their peripheral vision, thereby strengthening weak eye muscles. As with blind people, when one sense is handicapped the other senses are more fully exercised and developed.

How Much Can Very Young Children Do?

Question: Can young children concentrate for a whole hour? Don't they get tired?

Answer: Although they have a short attention span, young children also have unlimited amounts of energy. Motivate them to use this energy constructively. Be prepared to present as many as fifteen movement experiences within a one-hour session. Also, frequently vary the dynamics, location, and formation of the movement activities. (See "Discipline," page 8, and "How to Use the Book and Plan Your Lessons.")

Question: Can they hurt themselves?

Answer: It isn't likely. Their bodies are relatively pliable and they are closer to the ground than we are. They have an instinct for relaxing when falling. However, *never* force a child's taut body into a position. Instead, touch the child's body and suggest the position with gentle voice and hands. When the children reach a point near muscle strain, they will probably stop doing the exercise. Their bodies will be expressing their fatigue. Tune in to the group.

How Young?

Question: Can children start to learn to dance in nursery school?

Answer: Children certainly begin to dance at home. Many of them bounce and dance in response to music before they can walk. They can be stimulated at any age to appreciate the joys of dance.

Up to the age of four, children learn primarily through reflecting your movements and those of other children (see the Introduction to "Invisible Strings," page 92). They also learn a great deal from watching older children. If you move with joy—without insisting that they do it *your* way—they will move with you. They are not yet ready for the discipline of forms: circles, lines, "stay with your partner," "stay with the group." They are most comfortable moving as individuals. At about the age of four, they can begin to accept and enjoy movements that require social interaction and responsibility to a group.

I Feel Inadequate

There are days when I question whether I have any right to teach dance to children. Shouldn't I be a beautiful ballerina? Shouldn't I be the perfect model for the children to admire and want to emulate? Maybe I'm teaching them to be clumsy—or at best, mediocre? Maybe I'm doing more harm than good?

On days like these, I give myself a lecture. Our culture gives us many hang-ups. One of the most treacherous of these is the fear that we are somehow "exposing" ourselves when we move in front of other people. In addition, we grow up (especially women) with a fantasy ideal of what our bodies should look like—an ideal that *no* one can achieve. Consequently we cover, we hide, we change parts that somehow do not fit the fashion of the moment. At varying times, we all feel inadequate.

Relax. If you are a good teacher, you already have the basis for what it takes to use any art form as a medium for learning. Choose some of the beginning activities and try them out with your children. Encourage the children with: "How beautifully Lisa is doing that movement!" or "Look, Johnny found a new way to do it!" The children will respond with so much enthusiasm that they will stimulate you and force you to repeat and develop the experience. You will find yourself growing in confidence through their enthusiasm, becoming more and more involved.

In time, you will recognize the artist-teacher inside yourself, since the essence of the artist-teacher is to be a catalyst, an anchor, a force: to give, to love, to nurture, and to expand and help flower the potential of others. Of course, you can expect no Oscars or public acclaim for your artistry. However, you already know from your present teaching that the reward lies within you.

Imagery

Teachers often ask me why I use so much imagery—with adults as well as with children.

What is the value of imaging? It is the very source of the *imag*-ination. It takes us back to our earliest childhood memories. Before we learned to talk we thought in images. We learned to understand the world and ourselves through images. In our dreams, we communicate with ourselves through images. When we evoke images, we are exercising our imaginations. We are opening into a part of ourselves that bypasses and goes beyond the intellect.

I use imagery to help reawaken and rediscover our ability to be imaginative; to refind the magic and the children within us; to help us stay in touch with the childlike qualities of delight, honesty, immediacy, spontaneity, humor, and flexibility. Creating an image in class sets off a dynamic process. The image becomes a catalyst, calling forth spontaneously one image after another in a kind of domino effect. I might say, "This circle is a big balloon. What could happen to it?" One child may see it collapsing, one may see it getting larger, popping, or floating through space. Once we are involved with the image we are free to take it in any direction. It can teach us about spatial awareness, or about the relative values of time—when the wind blows hard, the balloon goes much faster; when the balloon has a tiny hole in it, it loses air very slowly. Any image can produce this domino effect. It's fun to experiment. Pick an image and see where it goes. When your imagination opens you will stimulate the children, just as their imaginations stimulate you.

Question: When *do* you use imagery for children?

Answer: When I want to involve the whole child. An image immediately conjures up an emotion. I find it particularly useful to use imagery for body techniques. When I say to a child, "Reach toward me; I have something you want very much," the child who is getting into a "Table Top" position from the floor will pull up her/his back and find the exact balancing point. Imagery provides a marvelous shortcut to the improvement of body techniques. Images motivate young children to give of themselves willingly and to put out physical effort that they would not otherwise exert. At the same time, they are unconsciously absorbing the knowledge that movement communicates.

Question: How do you choose an image?

Answer: If, for instance, I want to teach a specific body technique, I go through the movement myself and find that images come to me. Prob-ably I have been exercising this ability for a long time. What factors need to be present for an image to successfully motivate children?

The image must be *within the experience of the children*. Many midwestern children have never been in the ocean. Alaskan children know a great deal about seals, loggers, and snow.

The image should also be *appropriate to the age level of the children*. To accomplish a stomach-muscle exercise, very young children will respond to the "Playground Slides" image, while slightly older children will be more responsive to "Table Tops."

The image must be *within the cultural mores of the children*. If you are pretending to go on a picnic, pack the foods that represent the cultures of the children in your class.

The image must be *relevant to your goal*. If you are teaching the children to jump from a very low position to a very high one, rather than choosing a bunny rabbit, choose a kangaroo.

The image needs to *motivate the children* toward physical or emotional fulfillment, or toward both. If your goal is a torso stretch and your image is "Climbing a Ladder," your voice should urge the children to "climb higher . . . and higher!" They become so involved that they extend themselves farther than ever before. This brings a tremendous feeling of fulfillment within their bodies.

Other ways to find an image include asking the children, "What does this feel like? What could we be?" while they are actively moving. Music will also call forth images.

Question: Should I always work with images? Isn't it better for the children to create their own images? Should I simply say, "Make a shape"?

Answer: I don't think that my use of imagery discourages the children from developing their own imaginations. In fact, it seems to stimulate them. In a sense, I am giving them "permission" to be imaginative. However, providing an image is certainly not the only way to stimulate their imaginations. Movements like "Imaginary Props" and "Response to Environment" are specifically designed to stimulate them to create their own images. I think that if I said, "Make a shape," I'd quickly add, "How does that shape make you feel?" so that the image would evolve from an emotional association. Moving with imagery seems to involve the children totally, making their expression artistic.

Question: When *don't* I use imagery?

Answer: It's not wise to use imagery if there is a strong possibility that the children have little sense of reality. Children who are severely emotionally disturbed—who may be living entirely in a fantasy world—can be confused by the use of imagery.

I try to make it very clear with the normal child that we are *pretending*. I

remember one day when I was working toward good body alignment
with five-year-olds. We pretended
to make mud pies in pie tins. I suggested that we balance the mud pies
on our heads while we walked in
the sun. One little girl said, "Oh, I
can't do that. My mother just washed
my hair!" I quickly answered, "We're
just pretending. We wouldn't put
real mud pies on our heads, would
we?" She was relieved.

The Kinaesthetic Sense

Question: What is the *kinaesthetic sense?*

Answer: Dictionaries define *kinaesthesia* as the sensation of movement or strain in muscles, tendons, and joints (from the Greek *kinein*, "to move," and *aisthesis*, "perception").

The best way to understand and appreciate the importance of the kinaesthetic sense is to feel it functioning. Try this:

1. Put one hand behind your back. Do not touch your back.

2. You can readily recognize that without using your visual sense, you know that your hand is behind you. You can feel it in your muscles. If you hold it there long enough, you become aware of your bloodstream functioning. You are aware, from your shoulder to your finger tips, that your hand is *behind* and not in front of you. This body awareness of the space around you through the kinaesthetic sense is the basis of spatial awareness (see the "Spatial Awareness" section).

3. Change hands. Squeeze the hand that is behind your back into a tight fist . . . open it sharply and strongly . . . close it tightly . . . open it strongly. . . . Repeat the movement three or four times. Now open it softly, tenderly . . . close it softly, quietly . . . repeat this movement three or four times. The element that makes the difference between the two qualities

of movement is *energy.* By exerting a great deal of energy very suddenly, you perform a very strong and intense movement. When you exert a minimal amount of energy, allowing it to flow evenly, you produce a lyrical quality.

Quantities of energy and how they are used constitute an important part of kinaesthetic knowledge. Long before you started school, your body learned that you could not use the same amount of energy to lift a pencil that you used to lift a table. If you had done so, you would probably have fallen backwards. Experience,

through repeated experimentation, taught this to your body through your kinaesthetic sense. Kinaesthetic knowledge is stored in the body and mind.

In our culture few of us develop the kinaesthetic sense beyond life's necessities. Blind people, athletes, dancers, and trapeze artists must extend their kinaesthetic knowledge. As you develop your kinaesthetic sense you will experience an exhilaration, an excitement similar to that of a person whose vision has just been restored.

Laughter By The Audience

Question: Why do adults laugh when they see a child stumble? Why does it upset me so?

Answer: I suppose that I am identifying with the child. The child was not attempting to be humorous. S/he was deeply involved in a serious moment. The audience's laughter shocked the child into self-consciousness.

I do not feel that it is my place to analyze why an audience laughs. I can only help the children by anticipating the problem. When I introduce a program I ask the audience not to laugh unless it is clear that the child is attempting to amuse them. I generally say, "Your laughter is probably an expression of joyous response, but it can often be misinterpreted by the children. They may feel that they are being laughed *at*. Use applause rather than laughter."

The Magic Basket

Question: Every now and then I go blank. What should I do when I suddenly run out of ideas in the middle of a class?

Answer: One of my sure-fire rescue devices has been the magic basket. I'll suddenly say, "You know, every time I come to class, I bring with me a great big *magic basket!* What makes it magic is that I never know what's going to be inside. Would you like to know what's inside today?" I pantomime opening a huge basket.... "Wow! It's full of live baby animals!" I walk around the basket, peering inside.... "I see a baby kangaroo... and a baby elephant... and a snake... and a kitten... and a little baby bear." Sometimes the basket is full of balloons. "All the different colors of balloons... any color you can think of! And some colors you've never seen before!" My excitement at what I "see" involves the children. I usually ask them to whisper in my ear what color of balloon or what kind of animal they want. I take it out of the basket for them and soon we're launched into another movement experience. We could skip with the balloon or do a movement activity with the animal.

Once the children are familiar with the magic basket, I often ask them to suggest things that might be inside. Their unlimited imaginations lead us in many directions. The magic basket also comes to my rescue when I find myself with a shortage of materials. If some children have to do without a stuffed animal, I have them whisper what color, size, and kind of animal they want. I take it out of the basket, making these children feel cared for and special.

Make Mistakes

Mistakes lead to new solutions.
Mistakes open the doors to the
creative process. (Feel free to discard,
to change your movements—
they're yours.)

16

Motivating Boys

Question: How do you motivate boys to dance?

Answer: You have to prove to them that the activity is not "sissy." Tell them that these activities require greater strength than any sport, and will enhance their performance in sports. Here are some of my solutions to this problem:

Present physical challenges, such as "Leaps," "Giant Rubber Band Hinges," backward "Progressions," and "Table Tops."

Relate physical techniques to athletic needs. For instance, when you do the "Dinosaur" walk you are stretching your Achilles' tendons and calf muscles. Say, "Well-stretched Achilles' tendons and calf muscles help you jump higher."

Use images, such as engineers, clowns, or animals, that appeal to your specific group.

Teach the scientific terminology for body parts, such as "torso," "thigh muscles," and "peripheral vision."

Avoid terminology that boys associate with feminine movement, such as "graceful." Say, "Make your feet long" instead of "Point your toes."

Music And Silence

Question: The children love moving to music. Should I use it all the time?

Answer: For certain movement activities, silence works better than music. For instance, in "Magic Slides" and "Invisible Strings" the children are better able to "tune in" kinaesthetically to their partners when there is no outside force influencing or distracting them. They become much more deeply aware of their partners, and the experience becomes much more profound. Experiment from time to time with exercises you have always done to music. Say, "This time, let's see whether we can listen to each other's body rhythms" or "Watch everyone in the group to see if we can move together."

In addition to silence, try other sounds: voices chanting, percussion instruments, nature sounds, or industrial sounds. Try to discover which exercises work better with music and which work better without.

Noise In The Classroom

The need to occasionally make noise is a physical thing. Children doing "Birds in the Nest" (from "Group Sways") alternate noise and silence with self-discipline.

Open The Vistas

I know that the study of dance has affected every aspect of my life. How can I work so that I am consciously passing on this life-enriching art form to children? How can I offer them the very widest range of emotions, spaces, language, sounds, and colors? How can I give them an awareness of the limitless possibilities of their own potential?

When I work with emotional expression, I must cover the gamut from extreme joy to extreme sorrow; from extreme anger to extreme love. When I work with space, I must cover the gamut from the space within ourselves to the entire solar system. When I work with shapes, I must cover the gamut from the tiniest dot to the most complex geodesic dome. I must strive for strong contrasts in all aspects of the children's sound and movement experiences, so that they will become aware of the tremendous breadth and depth and splendor of the magnificent world into which they can reach out for fulfillment. I want them to learn that much gratification is theirs if they *extend* themselves. The whole universe is out there waiting for them.

Participation

Question: What do you do with children who just refuse to participate?

Answer: Much depends on the specific circumstance. I remember recently in a class of four- and five-year-olds, one little boy suddenly announced, "I'm tired." At that point three of his buddies immediately echoed him. I said, "That's okay, Michael. You go and sit against the wall and watch us while you rest. When Michael is all rested someone else will get a turn to rest." Within five minutes Michael was back in class and another boy sat down. By that time the others had forgotten about being "tired." Allowing children to sit out without company usually does the trick. It's not much fun being alone while everyone else is having a good time.

Performing

Question: Why do children love to perform? Do they have to get keyed up, full of tensions and self-consciousness? Something special seems to happen to them after they have completed a performance. What is it?

Answer: Performing is extremely valuable. I find that the children feel tense only when I am tense, when I become over-concerned with making a good impression.

From the child's point of view, a performance is an opportunity to integrate many experiences that were formerly fragmented, including various body techniques, spatial relationships (often the stage area is entirely different from the classroom area), ways of relating to one another, and aesthetic experiences. The children are learning to recognize the performer-audience relationship and to experience the organization of a performance. What the child has learned about relating to others is essential in organizing a smooth performance.

Performing also gives the children a chance to gain some objectivity about themselves, to see themselves as others see them. On the stage they become aware—as though looking into a mirror—of what the audi-

ence is seeing. They are taking responsibility for being the focus of attention. They are willing to expose themselves.

Performing also lets children be nurtured by the acceptance of a sympathetic peer and parent audience. The child, receiving the tremendous energy sent out by the audience, says, "I exist. I matter." After a performance, the children are always more confident, more integrated, more enthusiastic, and strongly motivated to continue their class work.

Physical Education And Dance Movement

Question: What's the difference between dance movement and physical education?

Answer: In recent years, physical education on the elementary level has come closer to dance movement. Nevertheless, its major focus remains in the areas of *motor skills,* which are physical skills and coordination based on movements that prepare the children for sports; and *teamwork,* where the goal is to train the individual to relate spatially and rhythmically to the group so the group will "win."

Dance movement, although it too concerns itself with physical techniques and spatial awareness, uses movements that are designed for aesthetic and emotional expression as well. Dance movement also draws on the psychological and imaginative world of the child and concerns itself with the individual's relationship to the group on an emotional and aesthetic level.

24

Pitfalls Of Repeating A Good Lesson

Question: Do you remember teaching a lesson that really thrilled you? Do you remember trying to teach the same lesson to another group and seeing it fail? Why didn't it work?

Answer: Maybe the problem was one of these.

Were you worn out? Had you used up your creative energy?

Had you decided what the results would be, so that you were steering the students towards your preconceived goals? Were you closed to the needs of the group?

Had a structure been developed from teaching the first class, so that you "knew" what the next "logical" step would be? Were you teaching by rote and not allowing your sensitivity to the new group to dictate the next developments?

What is necessary to re-create the original magic? I seem to need:

A general theme, with not too many preconceived specifics.

A relaxed giving of myself, allowing the lesson to evolve organically.

A tuning-in to each individual child as well as to the "group character" of the class.

Sincere enthusiasm, making me a teacher-participant.

An insistent desire to search out new forms, new sources, new approaches.

Process

Question: When it comes to dance movement, what do you mean by *process*?

Answer: If a child can learn to make a continuous effort, if s/he can feel, "I'm on my way," and if the eventual goal of perfection is never reached—then I am dealing with the concept of process.

When a child says, "I already know how to do a cartwheel," s/he is saying, "I have the *product*." I say, "Try it on the other side. . . . Now see if you can straighten your knees and point your toes. . . . Now see if you can do it with one hand . . . no hands. . . . Now do it with a partner, keeping exactly together. . . . Now put it into a dance. . . . What are you expressing?" There is no end, no product. Your own delight with the fact that the possibilities are limitless becomes contagious and communicates to the child that the process is what really matters.

Body movement is a wonderful way to teach children the excitement of the process of living. It becomes *physically* clear to them that life can be a constant adventure.

Right And Left Hemispheres

Question: What is the relation of the right and left hemispheres of the brain to movement?

Answer: We think differently with each side of the brain. The left hemisphere is used for cognitive, logical thinking. The right hemisphere is used for intuitive, creative, spontaneous thought.

Our culture and our educational system have developed the use of the left hemisphere, placing little value on creative thought. As a result, we tend to use the left side of the brain instead of the right when we want to move with spontaneity. How can we break through this conditioning? For me, one of the most effective means is to use a fast, rhythmic, insistent beat when I want to encourage spontaneous movement. For instance, when I do "Tree Shapes" with the children, I set up a rhythm that gives them just enough time to move from one shape to another, yet not enough time to go through a cerebral process between beats. Watching them carefully, I can tell by the halting, stuttering way in which some of them move that they are prejudging the next movement and inhibiting their bodies from flowing freely. If necessary, I increase the tempo. The insistent rhythmic beat becomes the authority that forces them to break through the conditioned patterns.

Rights
And
Lefts

Question: How do you teach children their right from their left?

Answer: The question should be "how and when?" So much damage has been done in this area. So many of us have grown up with deep feelings of inadequacy ("I'm uncoordinated. I must be stupid.") because some adult tried to teach us right from left with no regard for our individual readiness and with no awareness of how to motivate us to learn.

Decide ahead of time what the goal of a movement activity is. Teach right and left *only* when that is your specific goal. If an exercise has other goals but requires directional movements, use landmarks—"Go toward the window," "Use the hand near me," or "Start on the foot closest to your partner."

When you face the class and say, "Raise your right hand" while raising your own right hand, the children become confused. The remedy is to face the class and mirror their movement. When you say, "Raise your right hand," raise your *left* hand. To the precocious child who says, "That's your *left* hand, teacher," reply, "I know that, Johnny. I'm using my matching hand on purpose so I won't confuse the class."

When your goal is to teach right and left, do it in a gamelike way so

the learning is fun and will be retained. You might use "The Swimming Pool" or "Twirling with Scarf."

To give additional help to a child, lift that child's hand lovingly with both of yours, saying, "Johnny, this is your *right* hand." The child feels the muscular action in the right hand, while relaxing in response to the feeling of acceptance.

School Productions

Question: What's the secret to putting on a performance that is not amateurish?

Answer: What do we see when we watch most amateur performances? The children are easily distracted, waving at their parents, making inappropriate gestures, looking tense or laughing with self-consciousness. How can this be avoided?

When the children are captivated by the dramatic motivation; when they are freely expressing their fantasies, dreams, and thoughts; when they are tuning in to one another; and when they are *totally involved* with what they are feeling and doing—then their performance is harmonious. They are expressing a truth that comes very close to being a work of art.

Self-Discipline

Question: How can I help the children achieve self-discipline?

Answer: It troubles me that when we are having a discussion and I ask a question, the children feel required to raise their hands to answer. They should simply express their opinions, recognizing that they cannot be heard when someone else is talking. It troubles me when a child interrupts a discussion to ask permission to visit the bathroom. That child should feel trusted to leave and return quickly and quietly. What can I do to help promote self-discipline?

I must create the kind of exercises that *require* the children to take personal responsibility (examples: "Orchestra Leader," "Invisible Strings," "Slides in Rows," "Partner Leaps"). When two children are trying to accomplish the "Mirror Leap," the *magic* they feel at their occasional success motivates them to repeat the movement experience until they have mastered it. Through repetition to achieve a goal, they are developing self-discipline. Eventually, a self-disciplined attitude becomes a part of their entire personality.

I must not be "hung-up" with the usual public-school procedures. I must establish an atmosphere of mutual trust and respect.

I must assume that the children are capable of the task at hand.

I must take responsibility for the work's being on their level and being so fascinating that the children naturally focus and concentrate.

My ultimate goal as a teacher is for each child to be so self-disciplined that I am free to present a problem to the class and leave the room.

Self-Image

Question: Suppose the child says, "But I can't do it!"

Answer: Unfortunately, that child is implying that s/he cannot change. I encourage the children with, "Keep trying.... It's the trying that strengthens you.... Each time you do it, you get a little stronger. When you enjoy moving, you are beautiful!" When a child can *feel* the strength or stretch in her/his own body and *feel* her/his body becoming more flexible, articulate, and harmonious, that child *knows* that change is possible. Once this concept has been accepted, the child's image of herself/himself is no longer fixed. It has become malleable. Through the body, the child is learning that s/he can choose to change.

Should
I Dance
Too?

Sure, not to show them how but to
inspire them and to enjoy moving.

Slow Down —Time Is Our Friend

Question: How quickly can I expect the children to learn a particular movement, to reach a particular goal?

Answer: Learning is like growing— it's such an individual thing. What will help is to remember that there is an essential element in the learning process—*time.* I've noticed, over and over again, that when I don't pressure a child to accomplish something, when I allow *time* between repetitions of a movement experience, things begin to happen. Often the child who has been having difficulty with a particular concept will, a week later, suddenly understand it.

The biggest mistake I made when I first began teaching was to try to teach too much, too fast. Even now, I find that I am sometimes so excited about a new idea that I tend to rush the children. When I find that my own enthusiasm for the eventual goal has not yet been accepted by the children, that they simply have not had the time to absorb it, I pull back and tell myself to slow down.

We all need time between learning a concept and understanding it completely. It is only when we have integrated that concept into what we already know and related it to the other aspects of our lives that we can really absorb it. We need time to make it really ours. Time is our friend.

Straight Lines

Straight lines can be fences for the mind—when used merely to impose authority. When they are used functionally and aesthetically they can open vistas.

The Terminology Trap

Question: "Oh, is that what that's called?!! I've been doing that for years!"

Answer: Intuitively you've been using many educational concepts because you've been involved with the *whole* child. You've taken for granted that children must be helped to use both sides of their bodies in order to move harmoniously. Labels like "motor-perceptual learning" and "laterality" are terms that identify one small aspect of what you are doing. They are intended to facilitate communication. Unfortunately, when we designate a child as having a "laterality problem," we are putting that child into a category, sometimes leading us to forget that we must deal with the *whole* child.

At first I was quite intimidated by the glib way in which the "in" jargon was being used. Now I am very much troubled by the effect it has on the unsophisticated parent and the beginning teacher. Learn what the jargon means, but use it sparingly.

To The Ballet Teacher

Question: Can you really teach ballet in a public school?

Answer: Possibly, if you don't set yourself the goal of creating professional performers. Many elements of ballet technique have general value. Why shouldn't the children have the benefit of these? The key to using them successfully is to motivate the children with imagery that is on their level. Here are some exercises you can use:

"Marionettes"
"The Swimming Pool" and its Developments
"Centers of Light"
"Bounding Jumps"
"Twirling" and its Developments
"Leaps"

Touching

Question: I love so much to touch the children. Why don't some of them like to be touched? What can I do about that? What does it mean?

Answer: For many people touching or being touched is uncomfortable. Be patient with the child who is resisting. I usually say, "Maybe next time," leaving the door open for the child to change her/his mind. How-ever, you should recognize that touching is a basic human need; that orphaned infants have been known to die from lack of physical contact. Children often express this need with affectionate hugs or even by roughhousing. Children touch and accept touching when they trust a relationship.

Create a trusting environment. Create movement activities in which touching becomes a natural expression, as in:

   "Twirling"
   "Progressions"
   "Baby Kitten"
   "Orchestra Leader"
   "Pretending to Sleep"
   "Rocking"
   "Group Sways"

Warm-Ups

Question: Why do we need warm-ups, and what are good warm-up exercises for children? What kinds of things should we avoid?

Answer: The body functions best when the muscles and ligaments are warm. Injuries to the body are much more apt to occur when the body is cold. Professional athletes and dancers have found that it is safer to be too warm than too cold. They wear special clothing to keep warm. I find that I must frequently remind the children to avoid strenuous movements when they first enter a cold room with a cold floor. If your floor is cement and you are working barefooted, you must be especially careful. Because the children love their "Leaps," they often want to start class with them. I tell them, "You have to be careful with all kinds of jumps. Any movements in which your body leaves the floor and must land with its full weight can hurt you. That's why we always save these for the end of class."

There are many exercises in the book specifically designed as warm-ups. Other exercises, although designed to serve other needs, can also be used as warm-ups. Check the goals of the movement in question. If they include "warm-up," you are safe.

THE MOVEMENT ACTIVITIES

Body Techniques
Relating to Others
Spatial Awareness
Relaxation
Rhythm and Music

Emotional Expression
Original Choreography
Aesthetic Experiences
Progressions
From "Rainy Day Dances"

Body Techniques

Dinosaurs
Climbing a Ladder
Marionettes
The Swimming Pool
Licorice Candy
Giant Rubber
  Band Hinges
Partner Rowboats
The Merry-Go-Round
Table Tops
Playground Slides

Baby Kitten
The Rocking Cradle
Bridges and Snakes
Teaching Your Wings
  to Fly
Trees
Body Alignment
Centers of Light
Passing the Shoe
Calf Stretches

A knowledge of the world can only come from awareness. Awareness of the world—its space, its people—must begin with an awareness of one's self. Awareness of one's self begins with an awareness of the body—its parts, how it moves, and how it feels.

When we awaken our bodies through body techniques, we become aware of our muscles, joints, bloodstream, and breath. We learn to isolate body parts, thereby gaining control over them. We can choose to tense or relax, to jerk or to flow. When we have learned to discipline our bodies, we have learned a process for disciplining our lives. When we have developed an awareness of our bodies, we have found a process for becoming aware of others and of the world around us.

Dinosaurs

For:
Ages 4–10 (A)
Warm-up
Stretches:
 Hamstrings
 Achilles' tendon
 Calf muscles
 Back of neck

Teacher To Students:
"The Dinosaur Goes to School"

"You know that long ago there were animals called *dinosaurs.* I wonder if children dinosaurs had to go to school? What would they have to learn in school? It's possible that they had to learn the difference between their hands and their feet. Do you know the difference between your hands and your feet? That sounds like a silly question, but if you walked on both your hands and your feet, it would be hard to know the difference."

Teacher To Students:
"The Dinosaur Practices"

"Pretend that I'm the teacher and you are the dinosaur children. 'Stand up on two feet, children.' You're going to tap your hands in front of you as though you were tapping a drum. As you tap each hand, you will say, 'Hand, hand.' Then you will stamp your feet on the ground. As you stamp each foot you will say, 'Foot, foot.' . . . Let's practice it in rhythm. . . . 'Hand, hand, foot, foot; hand, hand, foot, foot.' Be sure that you are not moving your foot when you are saying the word *hand* and you are not moving your hand when you are saying the word *foot.* We'll keep practicing until we no longer get mixed up."

To The Teacher

The "Dinosaur" walk is flat footed and stiff legged. The whole foot and leg are lifted and placed onto the floor, so that the heel is always down.

Teacher To Students:
"The Dinosaur Walks and Talks"

"We're ready to learn to walk and talk. Put your hands on the floor. Keep your heels down and your knees straight. Walk forward saying, 'Hand, hand, foot, foot.' Move only your hand when you say, 'hand.' Move only your foot when you say, 'foot.' If you look through your legs, your head will be down and the back of your neck will be stretched."

DEVELOPMENT I: "THE HAPPY DINOSAUR GOES TO A PARTY"

Teacher To Students

"The dinosaurs have been working very hard at school. You're pretty proud of yourselves. You can keep your knees straight and your heels down (well, most of the time), and you know the difference between your hands and your feet. You're ready to take a long walk to go to a party. You're very happy and you add a little bounce to your dinosaur walk. It goes like this:

Hand, hand, foot, foot
Bounce, bounce, bounce, bounce
Hand, hand, foot, foot
Bounce, bounce, bounce, bounce

When you are saying the word 'bounce,' you stay in one place and bounce your heels up and down (on and off the floor) four times. It makes you feel good to be able to press your heels right into the ground as you keep your knees straight. Go all the way across the room until you get to the party."

Accompaniment: Side III, Band 1 (Israel)

Hints

Many of the children are not aware that they are straining and tensing their necks because they're trying to look ahead. Stand behind a particular child, bend down, and say, "Let me see your face, look at me, I want to see your beautiful smile," and s/he will drop her/his head.

Some children will have their feet so far from their hands that they will find it impossible to lower their heels to the ground. A good way to help such a child is to stand behind that child, put your hands under her/his body (just above the hip socket), and pull the hips upward. You will find that you have shortened the space between the feet and the hands. The child will find herself/himself in a much better position to tighten the knees and lower the heels.

It's best not to trouble the children with right hand and left hand until and unless they become so competent at the physical technique that there is no longer any other challenge for them. (See "Rights and Lefts," page 26.)

If there are girls who might be self-conscious about what they are wearing under their skirts, have them join the last group that moves across the room so there will be no one behind them. (See "Class Costume," page 252.)

Use the terms "hamstrings" and "Achilles' tendon." Children love to learn "adult" words.

Climbing a Ladder

For:
Ages 4–10 (A)
Warm-up
Torso stretch
Leg stretch

Teacher To Students:
Story

''You're a sailor. This is your first day on board a big ship. You've been working in the hot sun all day. Now it's time for you to climb up a rope ladder. You have to see how far you are from land. What's up on top of the rope ladder? Right! The crow's nest. But you got very sunburned—especially on your legs. It hurts to bend your knees, so you have to pull yourself up with only your arms.''

Teacher To Students:
Exercise

"Reach up to the first rung of the ladder with one hand.... Keep your heels on the floor.... Now with the other hand, reach to the next rung.... Go higher and higher. ...First one hand, then the other, climbing eight rungs.... Don't let your arms drop.... You have to keep getting higher. ...After eight stretches, rest your torso* by dropping your arms and head toward the floor.... Your knees can't bend, they hurt too much. Do eight bounces toward the floor.... Don't worry if you can't touch the floor yet.... Soon it will be easy.... Just trying to do it makes the leg muscles stretch.'' (Hint: make *torso* a new spelling word—not easily forgotten after feeling the stretch!)

To The Teacher

Encourage the children to continually reach higher and higher *without* lifting their heels. They are lengthening from hips to fingers to extend their torsos.

It's important for the children to really drop their heads, letting go of the tensions in the back of the neck. Touch the back of the neck of each child who needs to be made aware of the place that doesn't want to ''let go.''

Accompaniment: Side III, Band 1 (Israel)

Vary the rhythm by first doing eight torso stretches, then eight drop bounces, then four of each.

41

Marionettes

For:
Ages 4–10 (A)
Warm-up
Body alignment
Centering for balance
Strengthening
   the back muscles

Teacher To Students:
Rising to Half Toe (Relevé)

''You are marionettes.... Your feet are together, your arms are open to the sides, shoulder level.... You have a string tied to your head that goes all the way through that crack in the ceiling above you.... A puppet man is sitting up there on the roof holding the string. He says, 'Come on now. Stand up straight! Look in front of you.... I'm pulling the string on your head so hard that it makes your back stretch up very tall.... I'm pulling you taller.... Until you come all the way up to your toes.... And now I let you down very gently.' ... (Repeat this pattern about four times.)... 'This time I'm going to hold you up there on your toes.... I'm going to put a string on each hand and I'm going to pull your hands all the way over your head.... I'm pulling all three strings—your head string and both hand strings.... You're not having any trouble staying up there because I'm holding you up.... Stay there until we count aloud together, one—two—three—four—five—six—seven—eight!' ''

Teacher To Students:
Knee Bend (Plié)

''Please, Mr. Puppet Man, let me sit down.''

(As you say this, you and the children are bending both knees. Your voice is childlike.)

''He says, 'Straighten up!' ''

(As you say this, suddenly and harshly, you and the children straighten both knees. Your voice has a mock harshness. The children must know that you are pretending to be mean.)

''You say, 'Please, Mr. Puppet Man, I'm tired, I want to sit down!' ''

(Repeat the knee bend.)

''He says, 'Straighten up!' ''

''Gosh, he's mean!''

(Straighten knees.)

''You say, '*Please* let me sit down.' ''

(As you bend your knees this time, your face looks as though you are about to cry.)

''He says, 'Straighten up!' ''

(Straighten knees.)

''You say, '*Please*, Mr. Puppet Man!' ''

(This time your knees stay bent and your face and voice become an exaggerated cry.)

" 'Oh, all right,' he says. 'I'll let you sit down, but you must sit as though you are sitting on a straight-backed chair.' (Don't let your behind stick out.) 'Let's see how straight you can sit.' "

(The backs are straight. The hips are lined up under the shoulders to achieve good body alignment.)

"I'm still pulling your head string. Now straighten your knees."

(Your voice has become your own.)

"Let's do it again. Bend and feel as though the Puppet Man is pulling your head string while you sit on a very straight chair."

(Repeat the bending and straightening about three or four times as you help some individual children to feel the hip-under-shoulders alignment.)

"Let's shake out our legs to rest them."

(Shake each leg loosely from the hip and thigh.)

Hints

When the children become familiar with this exercise and its dramatic motivation, you can then use "The Puppet Man is pulling your strings" as a frame of reference when you need to correct their body alignment.

The knee bend can be done with the feet straight ahead or in "first position." In any case, the knees should always be bent *away*

from each other, so that an imaginary plumb line dropped from the knee would fall onto the middle toe. This position keeps the longitudinal arch* lifted and helps to strengthen it.

For greater ease in balancing, each child can place one hand on the back of a chair (as on a dancer's "barre").

Hints for the Ballet Teacher

Plié. "Marionettes" is an excellent motivation for "plié"* and "relevé." In preballet training for the very young, it is wise to open the toes only as far as the natural pelvic opening. On the "plié," saying, "Your knees go away from each other" helps to align them over the smallest toes.

Language. It's fun and enriching to say, "Do you know what language dancers use for ballet?... You can speak French, too.... Say, *relevé* (or *elevé*) every time the Puppet Man pulls you up. Say it together in rhythm."

45

The swimming pool

For:
Ages 4–10 (A)
Warm-up
Spatial awareness
Right-left orientation
ESL

To The Teacher

Set up a row of chairs to simulate a dancer's "barre."* Face the children and have them face you. Their movements become a mirror reflection of your movements (see "Rights and Lefts," page 26). When your *left* hand is on the barre, their *right* hands will be on the barre. The children are standing with their feet together, or in "first position."

1. Place an imaginary pool on the floor saying, "Let's put a little swimming pool next to us." (Be sure to put the "pool" next to the foot *away* from the barre.)

2. Slowly point your right foot (their left).... Your toe reaches into the "pool" as you say, "Point your big toe into the pool."

3. "Oooh, *it's ice cold*!!" Your voice takes on the surprise and shock of having unexpectedly touched ice-cold water and your foot springs back into place. The children imitate you. Repeat at least four times.

DON'T WATCH YOUR FEET

Learning to *feel* that your foot is directly behind you develops your kinaesthetic sense and spatial awareness.

46

4. The movement changes to leaving the pointed foot in the pool. Keep tapping the toe against the floor as you say, "Now we're used to the cold water.... Let's tap our toes in the water and make little splashes."

5. At this point, if your goal is to teach right-left orientation, say, "Do you know which foot is in the pool?... Yes, it's your left foot.... We can sing a song about that." Sing with the children,

Left   and   left,   I   left   my   toe,   I   left   my   toe in   O—hi—o.

6. In order to use the other foot, everyone turns around and places the left hand on the chair. You move to the other end of the room. Repeat the entire exercise. Say, "Turn yourself around.... Put the other hand on the barre.... Now the other foot can have a turn to point into the swimming pool.... Which foot is it this time?" Sing with the children,

Right and right and   right and right.   How   are   you? Oh,   I'm all right.

47

Teacher To Students:
Turning at the Barre

"You're holding the barre. Point your toe into the side pool.... Cross *that* foot over in front of the other foot.... Lift up onto the toes of both feet (relevé).... Put your other hand on the barre.... Take the first hand off of the barre.... And turn yourself around. ... Now you're facing the other side of the room. You're ready to give the other foot a turn."

The likelihood of success (especially for the very young) is greater if the child is expected to absorb only one concept at a time. The technique of turning smoothly at the barre should not be focused on until the children have become accustomed to all of the environmental references, such as "side," "pool," and "other foot gets a turn." In the process of turning at the barre, "Cross the foot over" is a new series of words and a new space orientation.

To The Ballet Teacher

Motivate the children to use a first position by saying, "Kiss your heels together" or "Open the book." In the early stages (before you are ready to focus on good body alignment), do not emphasize an extra-wide first position.

The image of pointing the *big* toe into the "pool" gives the child the motivation for the exaggerated stretch through the ankle and instep needed to achieve a good arch in the foot.

The important thing here is to motivate the child with the delight of the "story." You are gradually building into the child the joy and fulfillment of successful movement. In this way, the child is developing the self-discipline s/he will need later to want to work hard at the barre. At first, the primary concern is with the joy of movement and with giving the child an awareness of each side of the body.

For:
Ages 4–10 (A)
Foot articulation
Warm-up
ESL

DEVELOPMENT I: HEEL AND TOE

Teacher To Students

"The water feels very comfortable now.... Let's play in the water and sing a song."

Heel and toe and heel and toe, heel and toe and a—way we go.

"Let's turn around and give the other foot a turn to play in the water."

48

To The Teacher

The imaginary swimming pool is on the floor by the side of each child. The heel touches the floor, then the toes. After repeating on the other side, you say, "Let's do the opposite," touching the toe first, then the heel (see "Do the Opposite," page 9). With the opposite you sing,

The knees never bend during this exercise. This forces the articulation into the ankle. (Say, "The Puppet Man is pulling your strings" in order to achieve good body alignment.)

Accompaniment: If you cannot sing the music, speak the words rhythmically or use Side I, Band 1 (United States).

Toe and heel and toe and heel, toe and heel and ba—na—na peel.

For:
Hamstring stretch
Leg extension

DEVELOPMENT II: "SPLASH!"

Teacher To Students

"This time, we'll do a *big splash* with our *whole* leg.... Point your foot out to the side of the pool.... Get some water on your toe.... Then *splash* the water right over your head!"

To The Teacher

This is a high "kick" of the leg (ballet term: *grand battement*). It is done with a sharp explosion of energy. It can be done either four or eight times, then repeated on the other leg. Work on keeping the torso aligned ("The Puppet Man is still pulling up your head strings") as the leg lifts.

The same leg extensions can be repeated to the front. ("This time put your toe into the front pool. Splash the water in front of you over your head.") It can also be done to the back. ("Point your toe into the back pool and splash the water over your head. Remember, the Puppet Man is still pulling the string on your head, so your back is up straight.") With these motivations, the head and torso remain aligned. The standing knee should be straight.

For:
Ages 4 and up
Spatial awareness
Verbal-kinaesthetic
*   association*
Rhythm

DEVELOPMENT III: THREE POOLS

Teacher To Students

(The students are at the barre.)..."Let's put down three little swimming pools. ...Do it with me....(on the floor) One in front of us...one to the side of us...and one behind us....Close your eyes and point your big toe into the pool in front without looking....Now point into the side pool....Now the back pool....Now bring your feet together (the foot returns to its original position)....Good! Let's do it again and say the words together to make a rhythm. Say it with me." (Repeat the pattern four times.)

front and *side* and *back* and *together* and
front and *side* and *back* and *together* and
front and *side* and *back* and *together* and
front and *side* and *back* and *together.*

VERBAL AND KINAESTHETIC

The voice is part of the body. Labels are intellectual symbols.

Naming while doing integrates the child.

"Good! Turn around and give the other foot a turn.... The other hand holds the barre.... Your pools are already in place.... Close your eyes and find each pool once again."

To The Teacher

Repeat the pattern on the other side with the children saying the words rhythmically with the music and with you. Make your voice strong and rhythmic as you match the words to the correct position.

Hint

Once most of the children are saying the words and doing the movements rhythmically, you can help the child who is having difficulty. Bend down and gently place the child's foot to the *front ... side ... back ...* and *together,* to the rhythm of your voice. Ask the child to say the words aloud with you. Be patient. You may not get around to each child who needs help in one lesson. In time, over the year, each child who needs your help will get it.

Accompaniment: Voices in rhythm.

The music is the same as for "Heel and Toe"; however, for this exercise you take twice as long for each movement *(half time*)*. You are saying the words with enough time between movements to clearly establish the spatial direction.

To The Ballet Teacher

Say, "*front* and *side* and *back* into *first*" for first position.

Licorice Candy

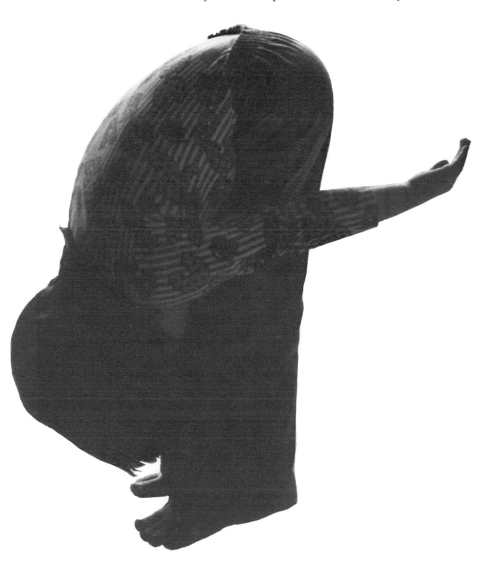

For:
Ages 3–10 (A)
Leg stretches
Warm-up

Teacher To Students

"I'm going to give everyone some pretend licorice candy today. Do you like licorice? . . . When I come to you, tell me what color of licorice you would like and I'll give you each a piece. . . . Stand with your feet together. . . . As I hand it to you, open your knees just a little bit, and slip one end of the licorice in between your knees. . . . If you keep your knees straight and hold the licorice tightly between your knees, it won't slip out. . . . When everyone has a piece of licorice, bend all the way forward and nibble on the licorice until your tongue can lick your knees. . . . Keep nibbling. . . . When you finish your licorice, stand tall again."

To The Teacher

Often I will ask, "Did you feel that stretch? . . . Where did it hurt?" At that point I sometimes say, "It's perfectly all right to say 'Ouch' when something hurts. Let's do it again and all of us say 'Ouch' together, in rhythm." Suddenly it becomes fun, and the children are more than willing to repeat the stretch.

Accompaniment

Use a fast, continuous drumbeat while saying, "Nibble, nibble, nibble, nibble," until you feel that the children have really stretched their hamstrings.

Giant Rubber Band Hinges

(suggested by Mady Taylor)

For:
Ages 4–10 (A)
Thigh and pelvic
  strength
Toe stretch
ESL

Teacher To Students:
(Motivation for Younger Students)

"Face a partner. Get high up on your knees. . . . Talk to each other and decide what color of *giant rubber band* you would like to have. . . . I'm going to get whatever you like out of the magic basket (see "The Magic Basket," page 15). When I come around, you tell me what color you want and I will put it around both partners. . . . One giant rubber band goes around the shoulders of *both* partners. . . . At first, the rubber band keeps you close together but . . . s—t—r—e—t—c—h your whole body away from your partner. . . . Tilt your pelvis and hold your weight in your buttock muscles, so you can be strong enough to stretch that rubber band backwards (if you let your hips drop, the rubber band will snap). The rubber band brings you back slowly and smoothly. . . . Don't let it snap you back. . . . Rock smoothly, backward and forward."

Teacher To Students:
(Motivation for Older Students)

"Do you know what a *hinge* is? . . . Where do you find hinges? Are there any in this room? . . . Let's see how they work. . . . Inside your body you have many joints that hinge. . . . Where? . . . Let's use the hinge joints in our knees. . . . Face a partner on your knees."

To The Teacher

Seen in profile, the "hinge" is a long, straight diagonal from the knees to the head. The pelvis is tilted; the back is straight. (See "Body Alignment," page 83.) The head is lined up with the back. The toes are pointed ("stretched" is a better word for the boys). When children are having difficulty with this pointed-toes position, there are usually two causes.

They may need more stretch in the instep area. Repeated practice will solve this.

Their pelvic muscles may not yet be strong enough to carry most of their body weight, resulting in too much pressure on the feet. When the children are encouraged to tighten their buttock muscles, the pelvic muscles are soon strengthened and the problem will disappear.

Hint

The children will tend to lift and tighten their shoulders while hinging backwards. Your suggestion "Make your neck long" will help them to lower and relax their shoulders. Tension is needed only in the pelvis and the thighs.

VARIATION: CURLED TOES

To The Teacher

Repeat the above exercise with the toes curled up and under. This becomes an excellent stretch for the back of the toes. We make a game of it by saying, ''Rock back four times.... The fourth time that the rubber band comes back, lift the whole rubber band up at the same time and stand on both feet.... Stay with each other.''

For:
Ages 6–10 (A)
Thigh and pelvic
stretch
Toe stretch
Group relationship

DEVELOPMENT I: GROUP CIRCLE HINGE

To The Teacher

The students are on their knees in a large circle. Their bodies are vertical from the knee to the top of the head. Their arms are lifted, fingers touching one another's. The toes are extended (pointed) behind them.

Teacher To Students

"Imagine that your arms are one big round giant rubber band.... Make the circle perfectly round.... As you hinge backward, you are s—t—r—e—t—·c—h—i—n—g the rubber band. Hinge slowly, using your peripheral vision* so the rubber band stays even and round.... Watch each other.... If you tilt your pelvis, the rubber band won't snap back.... Each time you return, your finger tips touch again."

To The Teacher

Repeat the curled-toes variation in this large circle formation. The motivation in this instance can be "After we have done four hinges, lift the entire rubber band at the same time, by touching finger tips and keeping the arms perfectly quiet.... We rise up to both feet gradually and together."

DEVELOPMENT II: COLLAPSED HINGE

Teacher To Students

"This time, we'll let the hips (pelvis) collapse. At the same time, we'll try to keep the rubber band perfectly round. Here are the counts:

One	Hinge back the way you did before (Development I), s—t—r—e—t—c—h—i—n—g the rubber band.
Two	Drop your hips (pelvis) so that you're sitting on your heels. (Your toes are pointed under you.)
Three	Keeping the rubber band round, lift your hips (pelvis) off your heels by tilting it forward and upward.
Four	Come all the way up to the original position."

Hints

The children will tend to drop their arms when they drop their hips. Reminding them to "hold the rubber band up" will help.

The children will show a strong tendency to lift and tense the shoulders as they try to lift the hips. Reminding them, "Make your neck long" will help to relax the shoulders.

Alternate Motivations

For very young children, the "Collapsed Hinge" can become a "Broken Rocking Chair," which the child proceeds to fix by lifting the pelvis to its original position (see *The Art of Learning through Movement* by Anne and Paul Barlin). The older children can become a large "Giant Balloon."

For:
Ages 7–12 (A)
Strength for thighs
and pelvis

DEVELOPMENT III: HAMMOCKS AND TREES

To The Teacher

The students are holding hands in a circle. Alternating around the circle, one student stands with feet together, the next with feet comfortably apart. (If necessary, you join the group to make an even number.) Suggest that they "hold hands gently."

Teacher To Students

"The people with their feet together are the *hammocks*. . . . The people with their feet apart are the *trees*."

To The Trees

"You are standing tall and strong. . . . Your arms are holding the swinging hammocks. . . . Do not swing your arms. . . . The hammocks will swing themselves."

To The Hammocks

"Instead of your arms swinging, your pelvis will swing.

1. Start in a bent-knee position. . . . Your heels are on the floor.

2. Your heels will lift off the floor as you bounce your buttocks down to your heels and . . .

3. swing your hips forward, lifting and tilting your pelvis up in front of you.

Return, by again bouncing your buttocks down to your heels and . . . swing your hips backward, lifting your pelvis back up to your original standing position."

To The Teacher

Repeat the forward and backward swings four times (eight beats). . . . Then the hammocks open their legs to become trees, while the trees close their legs to become hammocks.

Once the technique has been learned, it can be put into the following rhythmic form. Instead of doing the fourth backward swing, have the hammocks continue to lift forward in the pelvis until they are standing upright. They end that last swing with a jump; landing with their feet apart, they become trees. At the same time the trees jump, bringing their feet together as they

1

2

3

land to become hammocks. The new hammocks immediately bounce down into the forward and backward swings.

Hint

When the children are still developing their thigh strength, two phrases of eight beats is as much as can be expected.

DEVELOPMENT IV: BODY SUCCESSIONS

To The Teacher

This is a very sophisticated development of the thigh and pelvic strength movement. Use it only after the older students have shown a good deal of strength in those areas through exercises like "Hammocks and Trees."

Teacher To Students

"Hold hands in your circle formation. Every other person will move, just as you did in "Hammocks and Trees." The non-movers will support the movers."

Movers: Starting Position

"You are on half toe (heels are lifted off the floor).... Bend over forward, rounding your back with your head toward your

61

knees.... Bend your knees until your buttocks are close to your heels."

Movers: Movement

"Imagine that there is a wall directly in front of you.... Press your knees toward that wall (this action lifts your body slightly).... Press your pelvis toward that wall, lifting it forward and upward.... Your body is now slightly higher, as in the "hammock swing."... Your head remains forward and down.... Keep the pelvis pressing forward and upward as you imagine that someone has a string attached to your sternum (breastbone) and is pulling it. Lift your chest upward toward the ceiling (until now, you have been trying to keep your head down and forward).... Still pressing forward and upward in the pelvis, and also upward in the chest, imagine that someone has a string tied to your chin and is pulling it toward the ceiling. ... Your neck is now long.... You feel as though your chin is pulling your entire body upward.... Continue to tilt the pelvis and pull upward in the sternum."

Movers: Return

"Stay on half toe.... Bend forward, rounding your back.... Make the return to the starting position flow smoothly into the next body succession. Continue the flow from one succession into the other."

To The Teacher

Two body successions for each group seems to be what the children can handle.

Partner Rowboats

(suggested by Wendy King)

For:
Ages 7–12 (A)
Slow leg stretches
 with breath
Warm-up
Relaxation

Teacher To Students

"Sit back-to-back with a partner.... Open your legs wide.... Touch hips and shoulders.... Relax your arms on your legs.... Partner One, very, very slowly breathe *in* as you lie back on your partner's back.... Partner Two, breathe *out* as you lean forward.... Move only as the weight of your partner's back moves you.... Let your hands slowly slide down toward your feet. ... Then, Partner Two, breathe *in,* lifting your partner's back, and lean on your partner.... Partner One, breathe *out* slowly as you feel your partner lifting your back, then leaning on you."

To The Teacher

The key to this exercise is slow motion. Coordinating the breathing with the slow movement results in deep relaxation. When the body is deeply relaxed, it does not set up any resistance to the leg stretch. Allow gravity—the weight of the arms, head, and torso—to cause the stretch.

Accompaniment: Side III, Band 4 (France)

The Merry-Go-Round

For:
Ages 3–6 (A)
Strength for stomach
and back muscles

Teacher To Students

"Sit on the floor.... Bend your knees.... Lift your feet off the floor.... Put your baby into your lap.... Put your hands on the floor beside you.... Push yourself around and around with your hands.... You're a *merry-go-round*!... Now go the other way. ...Do you know what muscles you are making strong with this exercise?... Put the fingers of both hands a little below your belly button.... Now lift your feet off the floor.... Can you feel those stomach muscles tighten up?... That's what's getting strong!"

VARIATION: BABY ON YOUR BACK

Teacher To Students

"Lie on your stomach. . . . I'll put your baby on your back. . . . Push yourself around with your hands. . . . Your baby is really sitting on a *merry-go-round*! . . . Now go the other way. . . . If your baby falls off, I'll put it back on for you."

VARIATION

Teacher To Students

"Lie on your stomach. . . . Put your baby on the back part of your knees. . . . Bend your knees. . . . Push yourself around with your hands. . . . Now go the other way."

Accompaniment: Side II, Band 2 (Italy)

Table Tops

For:
Ages 6–12 (A)
Strength for:
abdominals
back
thighs

Teacher To Students

"Everyone sit with both knees bent as close to your chest as possible. . . . Your feet are off the floor, lifted as high as your knees. . . . If you stretch your toes long, you will be making a *table top* on which I can put my drum and it will be perfectly balanced. . . . It helps to reach both of your arms forward to keep your back up and hold your balance. . . . Try to hold your table top until I come around and put my drum on it to test you." (The lower leg must be parallel to the floor in order to achieve a good table top.)

DEVELOPMENT I: TABLE-TOP WAVES

Teacher To Students

"Lie on your backs with your feet pointing into the center of a circle. . . . Your arms are open, on the floor, in a line with your shoulders. . . . Imagine the whole circle is one great big wave coming up out of the ocean.

1. Lift both arms off the floor, reaching toward the center of the circle until you land in a table top.

2. Keep reaching your arms toward the center as you lie down slowly. . . . Come up four times and go down four times, without my counting for you.

3. I'll say the word "And" to start you. By watching each other you come up together and go down together . . . feeling like one big wave lifting out of the ocean. . . . Then lie down, returning to the ocean."

Accompaniment

With no music or sounds other than "And" to start them, you encourage the children to become aware of their relationship to the group and to become an integral part of it. The slow tempo results in better body techniques. Challenge the children to move together by saying, "No one tells a wave when to rise and when to go back into the ocean. . . . It just feels itself move with the slowest member of the group."

Hint

When a group is very large I find it better to create an informal circular arrangement than a perfect circle. An informal arrangement that allows everyone enough space and is also visually attractive for performance purposes can be achieved by suggesting: "Take space, everyone. . . . Stay where you are and everyone turn to face the center of the room. . . . Now lie down on your backs with your toes pointing toward the center."

DEVELOPMENT II: CREST OF THE WAVE

To The Teacher

At the end of the fourth table-top lift, the children straighten their knees, pointing their toes toward the ceiling.

Playground Slides

For:
Ages 4–6 (A)
Strength for:
  abdominals
  back
  thighs

Teacher To Students

"Pretend that you are a *playground slide*.... Sit on the floor and bend both knees up in front of you, as close to your chest as you can get them....From your knees down to your stretched (pointed) toes, you are the top part of the slide where the baby sits before sliding down (that's why your feet need to be as high as your knees).

1. Balance your baby on the flat part of the slide....Reach both arms out in front of you.

2. Straighten your legs and let your baby slide into your lap....Your arms keep reaching forward to help keep your back up and balance you.

3. Bend your knees again....Keep your stretched (pointed) toes as high as your knees....And return the baby to the top of the slide....Now do it again."

To The Teacher

Position 1 is the same as in "Table Tops."

For the "baby," a real doll or stuffed animal can be used. Children love to bring these to class. The children who don't have a "real" baby can whisper in your ear, telling you what kind of baby animal they would like. You then take it out of your "magic basket" (see page 15) for them.

In the beginning, the children may only be able to repeat this exercise four times. However, abdominal muscles* strengthen very quickly. Challenge the children to keep trying by asking them, "Put your finger tips on your tummies...way down low where your belly button is. Can you feel those muscles tighten up as you lift your feet?" They can really feel them working. They delight in this discovery.

Baby Kitten

For:
Ages 3–6 (A)
Isolation and
articulation of
back muscles
Verbal-movement
association
Warm-up

Teacher To Students

"Let's all make a circle on our hands and knees. . . . Make the circle big, because there's a great big tree in the middle. . . . Look up at the top of the tree. . . . What do you see? . . . Yes, a baby bird. . . . Ask the baby bird to come down and play with you. . . . How would a baby kitten say that? . . . 'Meow . . . meow!' . . . Does the bird come down? . . . No, he's afraid of the kitten. . . . But the kitten doesn't understand this. . . . He gets very impatient. . . . He says, 'Come down here right now! I want to play with you!' . . . How does a kitten say that? . . . 'Meow . . . meow!' . . . Does the bird come down? . . . No. . . . So the kitten gets very angry. . . . What does a kitten do with its back when it is very angry? . . . Everyone push hard with your hands against the floor and say, 'Round' as you round your backs. . . . Now look up at the bird, let your back go down, and say, 'Meow.' . . . Let's listen to each other and the music and say together, 'Round . . . and meow . . . and round . . . and meow . . . and round . . . and meow . . . and round . . . and meow.'

"The bird still doesn't come down, so the kitten decides to play with its friends. On your hands and knees, run around the circle, chasing your friend's tail." (Everyone goes in the same direction.)

"Now chase your own tail. . . . Try to catch it. . . . Go the other way.

"You're very tired of playing and you're very thirsty. . . . Drink some warm milk. . . . Curl up and go to sleep."

To The Teacher:
Helping the Child

Watch the children. A child who is having difficulty locating her/his back muscles will probably rock forward and back, or bend and straighten the elbows.

You can help by straddling the child and grasping the hips with the inside of your legs. Then,

1. Put one hand on the head and one on the stomach.

2. *"Round"*: Push the stomach in and up toward you. This lifts the back. At the same time, gently press the head downward.

3. *"Meow"*: Use the palm of the hand that was on the stomach to press down on the back, while the other hand lifts the head.

4. Saying, "Push hard with your hands against the floor" will probably keep the child's elbows from bending.

Hint

Check the position of the children's feet. They should be pointed (stretched) rather than curled.

Accompaniment: Side III, Band 2 (USSR)

After introducing the story, put on the record. The music starts with a slow section of four beats for "round" and four beats for "meow." The entire phrase is repeated eight times. The music for step two, where the baby kitten is chasing its friend's tail, is fast. There are twelve measures in all. Use about half of them for step two and the rest for step three, "chasing your own tail." The music then returns to the slow section for step four—"drink some milk" and "go to sleep."

ROUND:

Grasp the child's hips firmly between your legs.
With your right hand on the child's head,
gently press down. With your left hand on
the child's abdomen, gently pull upward.

MEOW:

Grasp the child's hips between your legs.
With your left hand on the child's back,
gently press down. With your right hand on
the child's head, gently lift upward.

The Rocking Cradle

Teacher To Students

"Lie on your stomach.... Hold your ankles behind you.... I'll put your baby animal on your back.... Rock forward and back.... If your baby falls off, I'll put it back on for you."

Accompaniment: Side II, Band 1 (USSR)

Bridges and Snakes

Teacher To Students

"Lie on your backs....Bend your knees....
Keep your feet on the floor....Put your
hands on the floor *over* your shoulders....
Push against the floor with your hands *and*
your feet. Your body is making a *bridge*!"

"Wow!...Look at Ali's bridge!...I wonder
if someone would like to be a snake and
wriggle under that high bridge?...You
have to stretch your body and arms really
long....Snakes move by wriggling their
bodies....When Ali gets too tired she's
going to come down....Don't get caught
under the bridge!"

To The Teacher

At first, many of the young children will
create the bridge with the tops of their
heads resting on the floor. In a short time
they will complain, "It hurts my head." I
generally stand over them, lift their bodies
from *under the shoulders* so the head comes
off the floor, and say, "The harder you
push with your hands, the stronger your
arms will get. When your arms are strong
enough, they will push so hard that your
head will come up—like this!" Often I have
to add, "Look down at your hands" to
release the strain in the neck. Check to see
that the feet are flat on the floor.

Hint

If the children persist in pulling themselves
forward with their hands on the snake
movement, suggest that they keep their arms
down at their sides as they wriggle.

Accompaniment: Side III, Band 1 (Israel)

Teaching Your Wings to Fly

To The Teacher

Do this exercise right after doing the "Birds in the Nest" story from "Group Sways." It flows beautifully when you say, "Those baby birds had better learn to fly, in case they ever get into trouble again."

Teacher To Students

"You're a baby bird, teaching your wings to fly....Stand up....Let your arms hang loosely at your sides....Your palms are touching the sides of your legs....Bend your elbows so that they are pointing away from your body to the side walls....Your hands are sliding up and still touching your body....Now bend your wrists and point them away from your body....Your fingers are still touching the sides of your body. ...Now lift your elbows just a tiny bit higher so that your fingers come away from your body....Lift your wrists....Then let your shoulders drop and let your arms float down....The movement is very small at first because the baby bird's wings are not very strong yet....We'll do it small three or four times until we can get those wings a little bit stronger....Now we can lift them a little higher...three or four times....And now, all the way up until the hands can come up as high as the shoulders."

To The Teacher

You will find that if the children really drop and relax their shoulders, their arms will flow downward very smoothly. Their wrists will point downward with the fingers lifting slightly upward as their arms get close to their bodies. The goal is to achieve a very smooth, flowing succession of movement in the arms. (See "Arm and Body Successions" in the Glossary.) You might also want to point out that the arm ("wing") is attached to the body at the "shoulder joint." Have the children press down through the shoulders as they lift their elbows. Your touching the top of their shoulders will remind them to relax.

DEVELOPMENT I:
FLOATING

Bending the knees as the ''wings'' come down and then straightening them as the arms float up involves the whole body in the feeling of rise and fall.

DEVELOPMENT II:
ONE WING
AND THEN THE OTHER

Alternate the arm movements by having one ''wing'' floating upward while the other is on its way down.

DEVELOPMENT III:
FLYING

When the wings have become strong enough, the bird is ready to fly. The children can improvise to the music, imagining themselves to be flying birds.

VARIATION

Fly with a scarf in each hand.

Accompaniment: Side III, Band 4 (France)

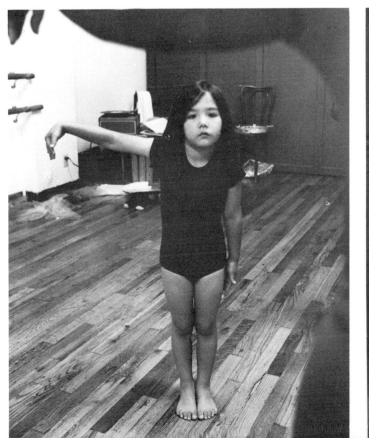

Trees

For:
Ages 4–10 (A)
Warm-up
Side torso stretches
Laterality
Group relationship
ESL

Teacher To Students:
"Trees in a Row"

"When I drive along a country road in California, I often see a long row of very tall trees. When I peek through between these tall trees, I see many many fruit trees—orange or lemon or tangerine....I say to myself, 'I wonder why that farmer planted those tall trees just outside his fruit orchard?' Do you have any idea?...To pro-

tect the fruit trees?...From what?...Yes, from the wind....Before fruit forms on the trees, there are blossoms. If those blossoms are blown off, no fruit will form."

Teacher To Students

"Pretend that you're a very tall eucalyptus tree (use any tree with which the children in your area are familiar)....Stretch your branches (arms) way over your head to make yourself very tall....Dig your roots (feet) deep into the earth to make yourself stand firmly....Your body is the strong tree trunk....Imagine that the wind is coming from the window side of the room; which way would the tree bend?...Before bending over, pull your branches and tree trunk very tall....Keep your tree trunk quiet and bend only your arms, head, and upper torso....Keep pulling upward as you bend. ...When the wind changes, you come back and pull upward again, growing tall, before bending to the side."

To The Teacher

The children are standing one behind the other in rows of six to ten children. Each stands at about arm's length from the child in front. Their feet are slightly apart.

For a clear designation of spatial direction, use a landmark such as "the window side" rather than "right" or "left." The goal here is the torso stretch and kinaesthetic awareness of the two sides of the body. It is best to focus on the body feelings with the image of the "wind blowing the tree from side to side" before concerning the child with "right" and "left."

Establish that the arms are "branches," the feet "roots," and the body a "tree trunk" to provide a frame of reference with which to motivate the children. If some children are drooping over to one side, sagging into the hips, you know that they are not getting a thorough torso stretch. Saying, "Stretch your branches very high over your head to make yourself very tall" encourages them to extend their torsos and lengthen their bodies from hips to fingers. When a child is thrown off balance by letting one foot come off the ground during the side stretch, suggest, "Dig your roots deep into the earth. These trees have been growing for a hundred years! Their roots are very deep and very strong!"

Doing this exercise correctly is hard work. You can expect the children to willingly do only about four stretches to each side.

Hint

If you have room for only one row at a time, the remainder of the class can sit and represent the blossoming fruit trees.

For:
Ages 7 and up

DEVELOPMENT I: ORCHARD OF TREES

Teacher To Students

"This time we'll have three rows of trees. Melinda, Greg, and Jacob will each be in the front of a row. Just you three, lift your arms like branches. With your head facing front, do you notice that you can see each other through the sides of your eyes?... Does anyone know what that's called?... Yes, *peripheral vision.** Melinda, Greg, and Jacob, see if you can use your peripheral vision and begin to bend slowly from one side to the other. Without my telling you which way to go, by watching each other you will be moving exactly together. *Move with the slowest tree.*

"Good! Now the whole class can do it. If the leaders are watching each other and are moving exactly with each other, then the rest of the group has simply to watch the person in front. I will say 'And' to start you off and then the whole class will be moving together. Just by watching you I will know which way the wind is blowing."

Body Alignment

A new term has appeared on the scene. What used to be called "posture" is now called "body alignment"—and for good reason. It is far more descriptive of the fact that in a correct standing position you can feel a straight vertical line rising from a point between your feet through the center of your pelvis, the center of your upper torso, and up through the center of your head. (See "Centers of Light," page 85.) Reversing the process, when you can imagine a plumb line dropped from the center of your head to the ground, landing between your feet—halfway between the toes and the heels—your body is "aligned." In order to achieve this, emphasis must be placed on the following steps.

Tilting the pelvis. The tilt is a rotation which simultaneously lifts the pubic bone upward toward the diaphragm and lowers the buttocks. (When you reverse the tilt, the buttocks poke out in back and the abdomen pokes out in front.) To the children I say, "Try to lift your belly button up to your chest." If I press downward on the child's lower back and press upward on the navel area simultaneously, the child responds.

Centering the ribs. In their anxiety to "stand up straight," children will frequently push the rib cage forward. For proper alignment, the ribs need to be placed over the pelvis. Although it is not an easy habit to break, the children can usually correct the problem if they can see themselves in profile. If not, create an exercise in which the children move their rib cages forward and back to develop flexibility and awareness.

Lengthening the back of the neck. Children will often lift their chins high in their effort to feel tall and lengthen their bodies. Saying, "Lengthen the *back* of your neck" helps to place the head in a centered position. Try a gentle upward stroke on the back of the child's neck. For very young children, the image of the Puppet Man's string pulling the child upward is effective. (See "Marionettes," page 42.)

Centering the weight. When standing on two feet, the weight should be felt equally on each foot. When standing on one foot, the weight shifts onto and centers over that foot.

CENTERED

Knowing where you are

Feeling your Center

Makes you Ready

Alert

Free to spring out

Without fear.

It's so easy to return

Because way out there, your

Center

Is

With

You.

Centers of Light

For:
Ages 7–12 (A)
Body alignment
  (posture)
Awareness of
  body centering
ESL

Teacher To Students

"You all know what an empty spool of thread looks like. . . . Can you picture a whole stack of spools, one on top of the other, with the holes matching?

"Pretend that:

1. The section of your leg from your feet to your knees is one empty spool of thread. . . . Stand your feet firmly on the ground.

2. From your knees to your hips is another spool of thread. . . . Put that onto the first spool, matching the holes.

3. Your hips (or pelvis) are another spool. . . . Put that one onto the two other spools.

4. From your waist to your shoulders is another empty spool. . . . Rest that one on the hip spool. . . . Leave your arms relaxed at your sides.

5. Your neck is a small spool. . . . Add that on top of the other spools.

6. Your head is the last spool of thread. . . . Place that on your neck spool, matching up the holes.

"Now imagine that someone is shining a flashlight from the top of your head spool through all of the holes, right down to your feet. . . . It makes a long, thin, straight line of light down the center of your body. . . . Can you feel the light? . . . It's warm, isn't it? . . . Walk around with the light inside of you, keeping it as long and as straight as you can."

To The Teacher

Often when children are told to "stand up straight" they will tense their shoulders and other body parts, throwing their bodies out of alignment. While doing the above exercise, you will notice that using a phrase like "*rest* the waist-to-shoulder spool on the hip spool" immediately releases the tension in the shoulders.

DEVELOPMENT I: IMPROVISE TO MUSIC

While the children are walking with the "line of light" in their bodies, put music on and make suggestions like:

"Try bending the line of light."

"Make curves of light."

"Try straight lines and curves on the floor."

"How about circles of light?"

"Maybe you can make your curved light go around someone else's straight line."

Passing the Shoe

Teacher To Students

(The children are standing in rows, about arm's length apart. There is a soft shoe on the floor in front of each row.) "Everyone bend over, pretending to pick up a shoe with both hands. Only the front person can pick up the real shoe. Let's demonstrate with one line at a time....Marie, hold the shoe in both hands in front of you and look at it....Reach up and lift the shoe very high....Continue looking at the shoe as you tilt your pelvis forward and look over your head to see the person behind you....When you can see Josh's eyes, you give him the shoe....Josh, you are standing with your arms in front of you. Don't take the shoe until you see Marie's eyes. ...Now it's your turn to lift high and pass the shoe....Marie, as soon as you finish passing the shoe, bend and hang forward to rest your back. Each of you bend over forward when you finish passing the shoe."

To The Teacher

The major purpose of this body technique is to develop back flexibility without weakening the back muscles and causing "lordosis curve."* (See "Back Problems," page 4.) The motivation "Lift the shoe high overhead and look at it" causes the children to extend and lengthen their torsos from their hips to their fingers. At the same time the child's weight is supported by the large

pelvic muscles. These combined actions take the pressure off of the spine.

When you work with the individual child, put one hand on the lower back as the other hand gently lifts the wrist. Be sure that the eyes are looking up at the shoe high overhead before the child bends backward.

The last child in line lifts the shoe overhead and drops it on the floor behind herself/himself. The whole line then turns around and repeats the exercise with a new leader.

Beware—some children will try to make a race out of getting the shoe to the back of the line. (See "Competition," page 6.)

VARIATION: SCARF OVER CHAIR

Teacher To Students

"Each of you has a scarf on the floor in front of you. . . . Bend forward with your knees straight and pick up the scarf with two hands. . . . Lift the scarf over your head very high. . . . Look at it. . . . Press your hips forward . . . bend your knees slightly and toss the scarf over your head onto the chair behind you."

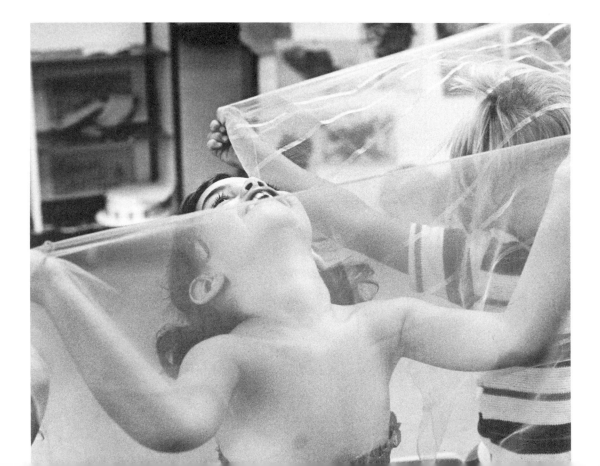

Calf Stretches

For:
Ages 7–12 (A)
Warm-up
*   for calf muscles*

Teacher To Students

''Your hands are on the wall (or barre, or back of a chair) in front of your face.... Your elbows are straight.... With your chest held high walk backwards, keeping your heels on the ground.... Press your pelvis forward toward the wall until you can feel the stretch in your calf muscles. Remain for half a minute in that position. Keeping the pelvis and chest high, bounce the heels on and off the floor.''

To The Teacher

This is a good warm-up exercise for the very beginning of a class—especially if you are working on cement floors. It is valuable just before jumps or leaps or any movements that require leaving the floor and landing on the feet. Also use calf stretches *after* doing many jumplike movements or movements that require being up on the toes. The stretches will relieve the tension that sometimes collects in the calf area.

To The Ballet Teacher

Calf-muscle stretches are useful after many ''relevés.''

Relating to Others

Invisible Strings
Child with a Kite

Invisible Strings

Introduction

On the surface "Invisible Strings" appears to be a simple exercise in which the children merely imitate each other. In fact, "Invisible Strings" is a profound and fundamental experience. Its source is the early relationship of the child with the mother. It recalls that first connection, in which the child reflects the sounds and gestures, rhythms and attitudes of the mother. It is the foundation for self-awareness and awareness of others.

In essence, two children reflecting each other are experiencing:

I am myself.

You are yourself.

We are learning to know each other.

You will observe:

Both partners moving in such harmony that their movements appear to be simultaneous.

Both partners so deeply tuned in to each other that all self-consciousness drops away. The result is a deep relaxation.

The initiator focusing so strongly on the movements of the partner that her/his body is saying:

"I am responsible to you, my reflection.

I must tune in to your abilities to move.

It is your arm that I am moving.

I care about you.

I feel your energy.

I feel your warmth.

I feel your movements reflecting me.

I feel myself expanding."

To The Teacher

We live in a culture in which "leader" connotes "the superior one," while "follower" connotes "the inferior one." The competitive movement relationship which results from this assumption is the antithesis of the "Invisible Strings" experience (see "Competition," page 6). In order to reverse this conditioned assumption, the greater responsibility is placed on the "initiator": the initiator must be sensitive to and aware of the abilities and needs of the "reflection." Changing their titles helps.

For:
Ages 6–12 (A)
Awareness of another
Concentration
Extending the
*   kinaesthetic sense*
Responsible leadership
Relaxation
Improvisation
ESL

Teacher To Students

"Would you like to see some magic?...
Amantha, face me.... I'm the *Initiator*.
I am tying an imaginary string on my wrist.
... I tie the other end of the string onto
your wrist.... You are my *Reflection*. ...
As I slowly lift my arm, I can feel it pulling
your arm up.... It really works!... Can
you feel it?... I can bring your arm down.
... I can move it to the side... slowly....
Let's tie another string onto the other wrist.
... Now I can move both your arms....
If I go slowly enough I can really feel that
we are tied to each other by *invisible strings.*
... Amantha, now it's your turn to be the
initiator.... You tie the strings.... Everyone
try it with a partner."

Hints

Suggest to the children that they stand far

enough apart so they can extend their arms
in front of them without touching.

When the initiator makes small, inward
movements (often an expression of self-
consciousness) the reflection giggles and
both partners become silly (see "Giggling,"
page 253). Whisper to the initiator, "Make
your arm movements very big. It will help
your partner to concentrate." Stand behind
her/him until you see the concentration
returning.

If the initiator is not able to feel the invisible-
strings image, try an additional image. "The
air is made of peanut butter. It's very heavy.
... Try to pull your partner's hand up
through it. Move very slowly."

Whenever you repeat a partner exercise,
suggest, "Choose a partner with whom
you have never done this exercise." This
way every child will eventually partner all
of the children in your class, taking care of
the child who is never chosen. All of the
children will find many new friends. It is
impossible to have a good reflection experience without finding something that you
like about your partner. It will be nurturing
to you, too, to find an opportunity to partner each member of your class.

Accompaniment: Side III, Band 4 (France)

Saying, "Start when the music starts"
helps to organize and quiet the class. Begin
by playing the music fairly loudly. When
the class is definitely concentrating, gradually lower the volume until the music is
almost inaudible. The quieter the music,
the more the children will focus on each
other. The children should also experience
doing "Invisible Strings" with no music.

For:
Ages 7–12 (A)
Music interpretation
Improvisation

DEVELOPMENT I: REFLECT THE MUSIC

Teacher To Students

"Take space.... Face in any direction... each of you works alone. Imagine that the *music* is your partner. The music is the *initiator*.... Your whole body is tied to the music with *invisible strings*. When the music goes up... let it lift you up.... When the music goes down... let it move you down.... If you can feel it growing strong and wide... you open strong and wide. When it gets small or narrow... you close in. If the music sways, you sway.... When it moves softly, you move the same way. You are being moved by the music.... If you like, you can close your eyes.... You can sit."

Accompaniment: Side III, Band 4 (France)

For:
Ages 7 and up

DEVELOPMENT II: CONVERSATION

Teacher To Students

"Do you know what a conversation is?... Yes, when people talk to each other.... Let's have a *movement conversation*.... I'll demonstrate with Jude.... I'm the initiator, Jude, and you are the reflection.... I move slowly, as though I am talking to you with my movement.... You are reflecting my movements as though you are listening to me.... Pretty soon, you want to answer me, so *you* become the initiator and *I* become

the reflection.... We haven't stopped to change.... Jude has smoothly taken over the initiative from me.... Then, when I feel, Jude, that you have done *your* sentence of movement, I again take over the initiative and you become the reflection.... We go back and forth, just the way a conversation does.... First I speak while you listen, then you speak while I listen.... There's only one rule: *only the reflection* can decide when it's time to become the initiator. ... Each time that you are the reflection, *you decide* to make the change.... If you stick to this rule, the conversation will flow smoothly, back and forth, back and forth."

To The Teacher

When the children have finished this exercise, they will naturally want to talk with each other verbally. Let this happen for a while. This kind of movement experience is a trigger that opens the way to verbal communication. After they have talked with their partners, the children may want to tell you how it felt to be the initiator and how it felt to be the reflection.

For:
Ages 8 and up

DEVELOPMENT III: FOLK CIRCLE

To The Teacher

Partners are facing each other in two concentric circles. One member of the couple is facing the center of the circles, the other member has her/his back to the center. The form is similar to that of a folk-dance circle of couples.

Teacher To Students

"Face your partner.... Drop your arms. ...Relax.... We won't decide ahead of time who will be the initiator and who will be the reflection.... Allow the music to play for a few seconds before moving.... Then, one of you decides to initiate.... The other becomes the reflection.... Continue moving in this way until I say 'Change.'... That is the signal for all of the people who are in the inside circle to move clockwise to the next person and stand in front of a new partner.... Everyone drop your arms again. ...Relax.... Allow a few seconds of music to go by.... Once again, without deciding ahead of time... one of you initiates, the other becomes the reflection.... Repeat the process whenever I say 'Change.'"

To The Teacher

Allow about thirty seconds for each couple to relate. A major value of this exercise is that the children have an opportunity to establish a deep relationship with a large portion of the class within a relatively short time.

Accompaniment: Side III, Band 4 (France)

For:
Ages 6–12 (A)
Dramatic involvement
Emotional expression
Verbal expression
of feelings
ESL

DEVELOPMENT IV: MOTIVATED INVISIBLE STRINGS

Teacher To Students:
"The Secret"

"We're going to do another invisible strings exercise. . . . Again, you will be moving at the same time as your partner. . . . However, this time the initiator's movements will be *motivated*. . . . What do you think *motivated* means? . . . Yes, it means there will be a reason for the movement. . . . It will have a meaning. . . . The motivation will be a secret between me and the initiators. . . . The reflections will guess the *secret motivation* after we're all finished. . . . Half of you come to me for the *secret*."

Teacher To The Initiators:
"The Secret Motivation"

(Whispered.) "Imagine that you have a very sick baby pet. . . . It could be any kind of pet. . . . Did you ever have a pet that was really sick? (The image of the sick baby pet "allows" the boys to express their tender feelings without embarrassment.) . . . What did you do for it? . . . What else could you do? . . . Suppose you had to wait before taking it to the vet? . . . Cover it? . . . Give it some medicine? . . . Hold it? . . . Pet it? . . . Give it some loving? . . . How would you *feel* if your pet were really sick—so sick that you thought it might die? . . . (Encourage the children to answer.) . . . Frightened? . . . Unhappy? . . . Sad? . . . Lonesome? . . . Worried?

. . . All right, when you go back to your partner, act out what you would do and how you would feel with your imaginary sick pet. . . . If you really live and feel what is happening, your partner will be able to guess. . . . Remember to move slowly so that your partner can stay with you. . . . Don't tell the *secret*. . . . Now join your partners."

To The Reflections

"Your partners will *initiate* a *secret motivation*. . . . You will *reflect*. . . . When you finish moving together, I will ask you two questions: 'What was the situation; what was happening?' and 'What were the feelings?' . . . While you are moving with your partner, keep those questions in mind. . . . If your partner is living and feeling the experience and you are really tuning in, it will be clear to you."

Accompaniment: Side III, Band 4 (France)

To The Teacher

When they have finished moving, everyone sits with you. Remind the group that each person's story will be somewhat different from the others', so they need not expect their guesses to correspond to others' guesses. Ask each guesser, "What was the situation?" . . . "What were the feelings?" . . . When you ask additional questions, you will find that the children receive far more information than they themselves

YOU CAN
EVEN TIE
YOURSELF
TO YOUR
SHADOW

realize. "Did it take place indoors or out?"
..."Just take a guess."..."Was it day-
time or night?"..."Was it hot or cold?"...
"Were you alone or were there other people
around?"..."Were you young or old?"

Make it clear to the guesser that her/his
story is as "right" as the initiator's, even if
it is different. Very often an initiator communicates images that s/he is not communicating consciously. Also, each of us
"listens" or *reflects* through our own experience. One story is as valid as another.

Other Motivations

Other motivations you can use for this
movement include:

> "You are four or five years old. You are
> lost in a jungle at night!"

> "You are a sailboat on a peaceful sea."

For:
Ages 7 and up
Inspiration for
*   creative writing*
ESL

Creative Writing

Students who are old enough can write
their interpretations of the story. The initiators write what they believe happened.
The reflections (guessers) write what *they*
believe happened. Then the partners ex-
change papers. Remind them to answer the
same two questions on their papers: "What
was the situation?" and "What were the feelings?" When the children have lived
through an experience and have become
aware of their emotional involvement, their
writing becomes more meaningful and
more poetic.

For the younger children who cannot yet
write, a painting of the experience with a
caption will work.

VARIATION: DUET IMPROVISATION

Repeat a previous motivation. Suggest,
"This time, after the reflection has moved
with the initiator's movements for a while,
the reflection can stop reflecting and can
join in the initiator's activity. For example,
if the initiator is taking care of the sick pet,
the reflection can participate in the caring
movements as a friend would. The reflection might hand the initiator a blanket with
which to cover the pet. The initiator might
hand the pet to the reflection to hold."
Both friends are now participating in the
improvisation.

Child with a Kite

For:
*Ages 6–10 (A)
Kinaesthetic
    relationship
Spatial awareness
Stretching the
    imagination
Interdisciplinary
    potential
Improvisation
ESL*

Teacher To Students

"Take partners.... One of you is holding an imaginary ball of string.... Tied to that string is a kite.... One of you is the kite.... What would happen if you let the string out?... What would happen if the wind blew the kite far over your head?... What would you do if you wanted the kite to fly high in the sky?... What else might happen to the kite?... Decide with your partner who will take which part.... You will take turns.... Use as much space as you can.... Be careful not to bump into someone else's kite.... Let's see what kind of adventures this kite might have."

To The Teacher

When you have completed the exercise, have the children tell about their "adventures" to the class. Hearing their classmates will encourage the others to stretch their imaginations. Following the discussion, reverse roles. After a while, you will find that the children love to "perform" this exercise for one another or for a program.

Hints

"Were you a special kind of kite?" is a question that can lead to a full discussion of the origins, varieties, and making of kites.

When this exercise is repeated, suggest that the children take new partners.

Accompaniment: Side IV, Band 1
(North Africa)

DEVELOPMENT I: CREATING ORIGINAL STUDIES

Teacher To Students

"When you do the 'Child with a Kite,' you have to watch each other carefully, so that the kite knows what the child is doing and the child knows what the kite is doing. ... You have to feel each other's movements.... What other kinds of things, animals, and people can you think of that depend on each other for the way in which they move?... One of you can be a leaf and the other the wind blowing that leaf. ... You could be a person doing something with an animal, or an object—like a ball or a swing.... Go somewhere with your partner and talk over an idea.... When you have decided on your idea, work it out with your partner.... Try the different movements that you could make.... In a little while each couple will show their movements to the class and we will guess what the idea behind them is."

To The Teacher

Watch the class as they work quietly. When most of the couples seem ready, call the class together for the "performance." If there are children who can't get going, suggest different possibilities. Some ideas that children have portrayed are:

The Moon and the Tides
The Sun and a Growing Flower
Fisherman and Fish
Child with Bouncing Ball
Child Pushing a Swing
A Tree in the Wind
Fire Burning a House
Child on a Trampoline
Kite Flying into a Forest Fire

For additional "Relating to Others" activities, see:

"Group Sways" page 124
"Tree Shapes" page 188
"Orchard of Trees" page 82
(Development of "Trees")
"Trees" page 80
"Listening Game" page 227
All the "Spatial Awareness" activities pages 104–120

"Take a new partner—someone with

whom you have never done this exercise"

develops flexibility in relating

to a variety of people. It also helps

the child who might feel that

"nobody ever chooses me."

Spatial Awareness

Take Space

To The Teacher

Having "a space of my own" is a luxury that not many children experience. Here is a simple way to have your children spread out throughout the room, using every bit of available space and having a space of their own. The delicious feeling of knowing "I am in the center of my own space" gives a child the freedom to move and the security to explore.

Teacher To Students

"I like to use the expression *take space....* Whenever I say these words, open your arms wide;...stand where you can do that without touching anyone....Keep your eyes open so you can see where you are going...turn yourself around...very slowly. ...Move into the biggest empty space you can find...very slowly, so your fingernails won't get into someone's eyes....Keep turning slowly, watching for the empty spaces. ...Everyone stop....Put your arms down and face me....You now have your own space in which you can move freely without hurting anyone."

To The Teacher

When you have become well acquainted with your students and aware of the fact that some of them tend to repeatedly place themselves in the same area of the room, suggest, "Mary, why don't you come down into this nice big empty space in the front?" or "Daniel, I will see you better if you stand in that big space on the side." Look for opportunities to offer new spatial relationships.

SPACE

Confidence is apparent
in the body of the child
who is comfortable in space.
Creating games that
challenge the child
to "do it backwards,"
"give the other leg a turn,"
or "turn the other way"
nurtures the child's
self-image.

The Choo-Choo Train

To The Teacher

Divide the class into short lines (four to seven children in each). Each child's hands rest on the waist of the child in front.

Teacher To Students

"The person in front is the engineer.... The person in the back is the caboose.... You will all have a chance to be engineers in this game.... Bend your knees slightly so that you can *scootch** your feet on the floor as you travel.... Listen to each other and make a choo-choo sound.... This is how the game is played.... Engineers, look for the largest empty spaces in the room.... Move into those spaces without ever going through anyone else's line.... If you see someone else going into a space, you must carefully change your track and find another large, empty space.... Try to keep the whole room filled, so that all of the trains are not piled up in one part of the room."

To The Teacher

Body and sound can be controlled. When you call, "Red light," the children stop moving and stop making their "choo-choo"

WHERE DO YOU LIKE TO STAND?

Some children want to be in the front. Some children choose to be in the back. Others prefer to lose themselves in the middle. Where a child places herself/himself in relation to the group is significant. Motivate the children to explore other possibilities.

sounds. When you call, "Green light," they resume movement and sound.

If the engineers are kept conscious of the spatial-awareness goal of the exercise, they are not likely to focus on speeding. Once

the group can do the basic movement, proceed to:

1. Move among the groups.... Whisper to the child who is approximately in the center of each line, "You are now an engineer." (You have just created two trains out of one.) By the time you have completed your rounds, there are twice as many "trains" finding their way around the room. Each engineer continues to be cautioned to "look for the empty spaces."

2. Repeat the above once again, splitting all the trains in half. In some cases, you may have a train composed of *only* an engineer.

3. Continue this process until the groups get so small that you say, "Now *everyone* is an engineer.... You are each moving on your own.... Watch the entire room to see where the biggest spaces are.... Use your peripheral vision to make sure you do not bump anyone."

Your goal is to have each child take individual responsibility for her/his own body in space. Each child is making constant decisions and adjustments to the continuous flow of other bodies in the surrounding space. In addition, each child is being asked to take responsibility for "filling the entire room," thereby accepting the needs of the group.

Accompaniment: Side I, Band 4 (Mexico)

The circle is a
very fulfilling form. It has no
beginning and no end. As pure form it
implies movement and flow. We first learned
about space by measuring with our bodies. As
babies, we reached out for our mother's hair and
learned to use our arm as a measuring tool with which to
comprehend the distance between our own body and an
outside object. A deep understanding of the space that exists
outside of ourselves must begin with an awareness of our
bodies' *being in* space. All of the body techniques help the children develop this individual body awareness. To help children
relate spatially to a group, I like to use the form of a circle.
Through the circle, the children become aware of themselves in
space *and* of their responsibility and unique contribution to the
whole group, because the circle elicits a flowing warmth, security, and wholeness. A child feels very comfortable in a circle. By
saying, "We need you to make this a good circle" and "You
can't make a circle all by yourself" you help the child understand that s/he belongs to the group while becoming
aware that s/he is a necessary part of it. Being part
of the creation of a circle and moving with that
circle give the children a sense of security
and fulfillment. They sense the connection with one another and the
space around them.

Creating a Circle

For:
Ages 4–12 (A)
Spatial awareness
Group relationship
Self-discipline
ESL

To The Teacher

Here are some of the problems that you might run into when suggesting, "Let's make a circle."

If the children are very young and you hold your arms open, they come running to hold *your* hands and there is no one to complete the other side of the circle.

If the children are slightly older, they run across the room to hold hands with their best friend—creating bedlam.

Sometimes the children take hands in a circle formation and begin to pull (with all of the girls on one side and all of the boys on the other).

These responses result in your losing time while you regain control of the group. Here is a simple solution.

To begin with, establish what size you want the circle to be, based on the size of the room and the size of the group. Do not mention to the children that you are in the process of creating a circle.

Teacher To Students

"Everyone *take space*.... I'm going to stand in the center of the room.... You stay where you are and turn your body to look at me.... Juanita, you are very close to me.... Look behind you.... Do you see the empty space between Lenore and Kristine?... Step back into that space.... Robert, you are too far away.... Look in front of you.... Do you see the space between Jeff and Mike?... Walk into that space.... Marie, you need to step back a little farther. ... Look behind you and fit yourself in between Koren and Dan.... Simon, you need to come in a little more.... We all have our arms down at our sides.... Good.... We now have a pretty good circle.... Without holding hands, look at the circle and make it as round as possible."

To The Teacher

Since you did not say, "Let's make a circle," the children are not functioning with any preconceived notions about where they will eventually be placed. As you use the children's names, suggesting that some need to move forward and some back, you are fitting them into the circle that you visualized in advance. As you proceed to place them, they will find themselves standing next to people whom they might not have chosen voluntarily.

You will find that the children accept this method of creating a circle, even after they have experienced it many times and are aware of your goals. It becomes apparent to them that it is the shape of the circle, the size of the room, and the place in which each of them happens to be standing that dictate who their neighbors will be. You did not plan that Marie would stand next to Simon. As long as you take their feelings into consideration by not insisting that they hold hands before they are ready, they will accept your goals.

DEVELOPMENT I: PERIPHERAL VISION

Teacher To Students

"Look at me standing in the center of the circle.... Keep your head facing this way. ...Do you notice that you can see the heads of the people on both sides of you at the same time?... That's called *peripheral vision.**...When you use your peripheral vision, you can put yourself right in the middle of the space between you and the people on both sides of you.... At the same time, you can see the whole circle." (For additional circle exercises see *The Art of Learning through Movement* by Anne and Paul Barlin.)

Hints

Because of previous conditioning, many children do not take personal responsibility for the creation of a good circle. They tend to blame other children for any defects in the circle's shape. They tell other children to "move out," "move in," or "move over." They even try to physically move someone into a new position. You can avoid these incidents by saying, "Keep your arms down and put *yourself* into the middle of your space.... If someone moves next to you, you may have to move.... If we all keep fitting ourselves in, then the whole circle will become beautifully round.... Let's give each person a chance to learn how to do this." In this way, no one feels unduly criticized. At the same time, the child who expects the entire circle to adjust to her/him is also being asked to be responsible to the group.

If your space is limited make two circles, one inside the other.

Don't be surprised if your circle insists on becoming an oval in a long, narrow room.

Balloon in a Hurricane

For:
Ages 4–12 (A)
Spatial awareness
Group relationship
Control and release
of energy
Improving self-image
ESL

Teacher To Students

"Without holding hands, make a small circle around Johnny so that each of you is touching someone on both sides of you.... Johnny, pretend that the circle is a big, round balloon.... You blow it up.... Blow.... Blow.... Blow.... What's happening to the circle?...Yes, it's getting bigger and bigger.... Remember to keep the balloon very round.... Blow.... Blow.... Blow. ...What do you think will happen when the balloon gets too big?...Right!...It will burst!...When you hear me hit the drum, that means that the balloon has burst.... Imagine that you are outside and a great big hurricane is blowing!...Each one of you becomes a little piece of balloon being blown all over the room!...Fly up in the air and fall down on the ground.... Twirl around and around.... Leap and roll on

114

the floor. . . . Keep on being blown all over the place until you hear this rattle on the tambourine. . . . That's the signal for you to come back quickly and make a new balloon. . . . Johnny, keep blowing until you hear my drumbeat.''

To The Teacher

As the children are opening the circle, say, ''Patti, use your peripheral vision* to keep the circle round.'' Make suggestions only occasionally, so as not to interrupt the flow of dramatic involvement. Since the

children love repeating this activity, there will be lots of opportunities for the ''round circle'' concept to be absorbed.

Give many children the opportunity to be in the center to blow up the balloon. This role is a wonderful self-image builder.

The children tend to return to the same place in the circle each time. In order to keep them open and flexible about quickly adjusting to new relationships, suggest, ''You can be anywhere in the circle. . . . If you go to the nearest place, we will form the balloon much sooner.''

If crowding occurs during the formation of the circle, ask the children, "How do you make room for somebody?" This usually makes them realize that they must step back, open out, and be aware of others' space needs.

DEVELOPMENT I: THE NOISY HURRICANE

Teacher To Students

"The next time the balloon bursts, in addition to your bodies' flying all over the place, your voices will also fly.... You can scream; you can laugh.... What other sounds can you make?... Yes, you can cough; you can yodel; you can gargle; or sneeze; or grunt; or whistle.... Try many different sounds, just as you're doing many different movements.... Keep making the sounds and movements until you hear the signal.... Then return to the circle and make a quiet, new balloon."

To The Teacher

Again, you have complete control over the amount of free movement and noise you can tolerate. You signal the children to return to the quiet circle when you feel the need. (If the noise brings the principal to your door, don't worry. By the time he arrives, you are busily blowing up the balloon again. He is sure to move on, certain that the noise came from somewhere else. If he should remain to watch, he will probably be impressed by the amount of control you have over your class.)

Exercising Peripheral Vision

For:
Ages 4–12 (A)
Spatial awareness
Group relationship
ESL

(These exercises are best done after the children have experienced "Balloon in a Hurricane.")

Teacher To Students

"Start with a large circle.... Your arms are down.... Use your peripheral vision to make the circle round.... Bend your knees and take small *scootchy** steps toward the center until someone touches you on both sides.... Check and see how round the circle is.... Now scootch backwards and make the circle larger.... Keep using your peripheral vision to keep yourself in the center of your own space."

DEVELOPMENT I: FINDING THE RADIUS

Teacher To Students

"You're standing in the large circle.... Your arms are down.... Use your peripheral vision to make the circle round.... I'm in the middle.... Look at me as I turn to you. ...Do you know what you call the line that goes from me to you?...Yes, the *radius.**...In a good circle, does the radius have to be the same length between Mark and me as it is between Frances and me?...As I slowly turn, fix your position so that your radius is the same as everyone else's."

117

Moving Circles

For:
Ages 6–12 (A)
Spatial awareness
Group relationship
Self-image growth

To The Teacher:
Preparation

Stand in the middle of a small circle. The children's arms are down by their sides. Their bodies are touching, shoulder to shoulder.

Teacher To Students

"Try to keep me in the middle of our circle.... I'm going to move very slowly anywhere in the room.... You move the whole circle with me, keeping it round.... Keep me in the middle.... Stay close to each other... so the whole circle moves at the same time."

To The Teacher

You are moving around the room, watching to see that the entire group stays with you. Your knees are slightly bent. Your feet stay close to the ground. Move slowly backward ... sideways ... forward. Try to change direction frequently enough to keep surprising the children, yet slowly enough for them to succeed. Moving too quickly could create a feeling of failure and frustration on their part. Your intention is to surprise them in a delightful way.

VARIATION: CHILD POWER

Give different members of the group an opportunity to be the center of the circle. The center child experiences a marvelous feeling of power when s/he can move a whole group in any direction. It is an excellent opportunity to give the shy child a chance to fulfill leadership needs.

DEVELOPMENT I: TILT-A-WHIRL

Divide the class into small circles of approximately six to eight children. Designate a "center" for each circle.

Teacher To Students

"All of the circles are going to move at the same time. Keep close to each other in your individual circles, touching shoulders.... Keep your center in the middle, no matter where s/he goes."

To The Centers

"Watch all of the other 'centers' so you won't bump into the other circles.... Travel slowly.... Move into the big empty spaces in the room."

DEVELOPMENT II: ROTATING CIRCLE
Teacher To Students

"I'm going to be the 'center' of your circle. ... This time, I'm going to look into Kiri's eyes and she will look at me.... I will turn myself slowly in place and the whole circle will have to rotate so that Kiri and I can continue to look into each

other's eyes.... I will go slowly enough so that you will be able to move the whole circle around."

To The Teacher

After you have demonstrated this Development, the children can have turns being "center." Once they become skilled with this Development, add it to the "Tilt-A-Whirl" Development.

For additional "Spatial Awareness" activities, see:

"Slides" page 202
"Leaps" page 235
"Trees" page 80
"Child with a Kite" page 102
"Three Pools" page 51
  (Development of "The Swimming Pool")
"Listening Game" page 227

Relaxation

Pretending to Sleep
Group Sways
Rocking

Children today are displaying an inordinate amount of tension. Obvious body signs of this tension are lifted shoulders, tight facial expressions, clenched fists, tight knees, stiff necks, and rigid backs. Movements performed under tension appear awkward, jerky, and uncoordinated. The tense child's breathing is uneven, shallow, and labored. When we can recognize these signs of tension, we are less likely to label a child "clutsy," "awkward," or "uncoordinated."

Dance-movement class is the ideal place for relieving tension. The following "Relaxation" activities are specifically designed for this purpose.

Observe your children in all of their physical activities. When all unnecessary tension has been released, the child moves in total harmony. All of the body parts are integrated, and flow with the child's intention.

Although important for all children, relaxation exercises are especially valuable for hyperactive children, who seem to have motors inside their bodies that cannot be turned off. This causes stress and dissipation of energy. We can motivate them to move slowly and quietly, helping them calm down and feel peace.

Pretending to Sleep

For:
Ages 3–10 (A)
Relaxation
ESL

Teacher To Students

"Lie on your backs and pretend that you're fast asleep.... I'm going to come around and see if you really *are* asleep.... I'm going to lift one hand.... And then I'll let go.... Let's see if it drops to the floor.... Then I'll lift your knee.... Let me lift it for you.... Let's try your long hair.... Sure enough, it's fast asleep.... I wonder if your shirt is asleep too."

To The Teacher

As you lift a child's arm at the wrist or elbow, you can feel whether or not the child is letting you do the lifting. If the child is consciously doing the lifting, encourage her/him by saying, "Let me do it for you." Sometimes a very gentle shake of the arm, while holding the fingers, will help to release the tension. Some children are afraid to trust anyone enough to let go of the control of their bodies. In time, with your gentleness and reassurance, they will gain confidence.

Hint

It is unwise to lift the child's foot, because her/his heel could be hurt by the sudden drop to the floor. Instead, lift the leg from underneath the knee.

Accompaniment: Side III, Band 4 (France)

Group Sways

For:
Ages 3–6 (A)
Group relationships
Voice and body
  involvement
ESL

Teacher To Students:
"Birds in the Nest"

"You are all baby birds....I am the grandma bird (or the mother, or the father). ...Let's all come close into our nest....I am babysitting because the mommy and daddy birds are out getting food for the babies....What kind of food are they looking for?...Worms?...Seeds?...We're nice and cozy in our nest, way up in the tree. ...A little breeze makes us sway with each other....The wind gets a little stronger.... Suddenly, the whole nest turns over and all of the baby birds fall out....Flap your wings very hard and fly all over the place, chirping, 'tweet, tweet...tweet, tweet.' The mommy and daddy hear the babies and come flying back. With the grandma, they put all of the babies back into the nest....The grandma says, 'It's okay now. ...Everything is fine again....I'll take care of the babies while you go out and get

some food.' . . . The mommy and daddy go flying off again. . . . We get cozy and sway together. . . . Pretty soon the wind gets stronger." (Repeat the swaying and flying and chirping process three times. After the children have returned to the nest for the third time, the story changes.) "This time the mommy and daddy bring back food. . . . Do you know how they feed their babies? . . . I'll show you. . . . Each little bird gets to take a worm from my mouth. . . . It's like getting a kiss." (A delightful experience.)

To The Teacher

The "noise" needn't present a problem because it is readily controlled through your "signals" and involvement in the dramatic motivations. Whispering (as they return to the nest), "The little birds are very quiet and cozy, getting ready to take a nap after all that flying" will set the mood for complete silence. Soon the children catch on to the fact that the flying and the tweeting will be

DADDY CAN ALSO FEED THE BABY BIRDS

"TWEET, TWEET... TWEET, TWEET"

repeated after they have quietly swayed for a while. They anticipate the change and delight in the contrast between their loud sounds and the total silence.

Hint

A good follow-up exercise after "Birds in the Nest" is "Teaching Your Wings to Fly." It is easily motivated by saying, "We had better teach our wings to fly, so that the next time our nest turns over we won't be so frightened."

Accompaniment: Side III, Band 3 (USSR)

The music alternates between the quiet, relaxed sway and the active, noisy "tweet." It ends just before the final feeding of the birds. The silence gives you all the time you will need to feed each bird.

VARIATION: SHEEP ON A TRAIN

Teacher To Students

"Face me and stand close together.... You are sheep packed into a train, being taken somewhere to have your wool sheared. ... Your feet are apart—just enough so you will be able to sway from side to side when the train starts.... Now we close the rolling doors and the train begins to move. ... Bend one knee.... Slowly.... And then the other.... Be sure you are going the same way as everyone else.... Put your hand on the shoulder of someone who is standing in front of you or beside you. ... Try closing your eyes and feeling which way the group is going.... Sway.... Sway.... When I hit the drum, the train stops suddenly.... The doors roll open! ... The sheep roll all over the tracks, in all directions!... Cry like sheep—'baa...baa ...baa.'... Keep rolling.... Guess what? ... The engineer made a mistake.... S/he didn't have to stop.... The engineer's help- ers put all the sheep back into the train... close together.... We're ready to close the doors again.... The train starts up.... Touch someone.... Close your eyes.... And feel the group begin to sway.... Try to move with the group."

To The Teacher

Repeat the group sway and the "rolling all over the tracks" movements at least three or four times. After the children have re- turned to the sway for the last time, say, "The next time you come back to the group, try to find a different place.... If you were in the back before, go to the front of the group.... If you were on the outside, go to the inside.... If you were in the front, go to the back.... Keep changing your place every time you return to the group."

Accompaniment: Side III, Band 3 (USSR)

For:
Ages 3–10 (A)

Other Motivations

Other motivations you can use for this movement activity include:

Each child is a piece of confetti inside a piñata. The piñata is broken and the wind blows the confetti all over the place. The sounds can be those of the wind blowing.

The children are crowded into a lifeboat. The boat capsizes and everyone splashes around in the water. The sounds can be the splashing and the screams for help. The children are then rescued and returned to the lifeboat.

Feathers floating from a bursting pillow.

Get suggestions from the children.

hand on the shoulder of the person in front of you and join the swaying line.... Now a third group of eight comes up and stands behind the second line.... Put your hand on the shoulder of the person in front of you and join the swaying groups. ...Now a fourth group....Now the whole class is swaying together.... You can all open your eyes and enjoy it."

Accompaniment:

Explore the use of both silence and music.

Hint

Music teachers will find this a beautiful way to get a group to enjoy singing in unison.

For:
Ages 6–12 (A)

DEVELOPMENT I: LINES IN UNISON

To The Teacher

The children are in a line, side by side (approximately eight children per line). They can either hold hands or each child can place a hand on the shoulder of the next child. They then close their eyes and sway together.

Teacher To Students

"You continue your sway while eight more children come up and stand in a second line behind the first group.... You put one

DEVELOPMENT II: ALTERNATING LINES

Teacher To Students

"This time, with your eyes open and your arms down by your sides, line Number Two, see if you can sway in the opposite direction from line Number One.... Now, line Number Four, go opposite to line Number Three.... Now, line Number Six, go opposite to line Number Five."

Rocking

For:
Ages 3–9
Relaxation

Teacher To Students

"You're lying on your backs....I'm going to rock you to sleep....When I lift you, let your head fall backwards, down toward the floor."

To The Teacher

Straddle one of the children, holding both wrists in your hands. Gently shake the child's arms to help release tension. Lift the child's arms high enough so the shoulders are off the ground. Swing the child's upper torso from side to side in a smooth, steady rhythm. Encourage the child with, "Let your head fall all the way back...I'll hold you." After five or six sways, allow the child's body to sink softly onto the floor. First the head touches...then the neck... the shoulders...and finally the arms.

Hints

Some children will lift the entire pelvis. Correct this by saying, "Sit down on the floor."

After rocking and lowering the child back down to the floor, softly touch the child's closed eyes with your palms before slowly and quietly moving to the next child.

Accompaniment: Side III, Band 4 (France)

The band on the accompanying record may not be long enough for the entire class. Repeat it if possible or find a soft lullaby on a long-playing record. I strongly recommend "Goodnight Song," written by Patty Zeitlin and recorded by Marcia Berman and Patty Zeitlin on the album "I'm Not Small," available on Activity Records from Educational Activities, Inc.

For additional "Relaxation" activities, see:

"Invisible Strings" page 92
"Moving Colors" page 162
"Partner Rowboats" page 64

See also "Swaying with a Pole," "Balancing Partners," and "Melting Snowman" from *The Art of Learning through Movement* by Anne and Paul Barlin.

Rhythm and Music

Rhythm Game in Seats
Clapping Orchestra
Orchestra Leader
Meter
Swing Your Arms
Cuckoo in the Woods

LEARNING IS GROWING

They were growing before we taught them
They were learning before we taught them
Growing and Learning
Learning and Growing
The drive is the same
Instinctive
Watch them at play: Hop Scotch
                    Jump Rope
                    Hide and Seek
                    "Who Stole the Cookies?"
The games they create teach them to balance
                                  to count
                                  to measure space
                                  to share
                                  to move rhythmically
                                  to invent languages
                                  to coordinate physically
                                  to protect themselves

Rhythm Game in Seats

For:
All ages
Rhythm with minimum movement
Audience participation (adults included)

Teacher To Students

"Let's play a listening game.... When you hear this drumbeat (play what you feel to be a marching rhythm), clap your hands. ...Good!...Now listen to this one (play exactly *twice* as fast as the marching rhythm).... When you hear that, wag your heads from side to side, like a waving flag.... Get each ear down to the shoulder, so you get a good neck stretch.... Let's practice.... Good!...Now see if you can change when I change. (Alternate the two beats. Make the change an unexpected one, but wait for the group to succeed.)... Here is a new beat (play *half* as fast as the marching rhythm).... To this one we'll all say, '*gi*—ant, *gi*—ant, *gi*—ant, *gi*—ant.' (Since the beat takes twice as long as the marching rhythm, you are playing on only the *first* syllable of the word.)...Let's practice that.... (When you feel sure that they have this, shift unexpectedly to one of the other beats. Then keep shifting back and forth among all three beats. Be sure that most of the group is with you before changing to the next beat. By this time, they have caught the spirit of the game.) ...Do you think you can handle a fourth beat?...Okay, let's try.... When I play this, you tap your toes—just your toes, because so many pairs of shoes will make too loud a sound and we won't be able to hear when I change to another beat. Tap them on the floor in front of you." (Play a beat that is twice as fast as the head movement or four times as fast as the marching rhythm. If you're using a stick with a drum, practice this technique on your own for a while. It requires a loose wrist. If you are using a tambourine, hold it high and shake it. When the children have caught on, change unexpectedly from one beat to another.)

To The Teacher

Whenever you want the group to stop, use the "stop" gesture (hands in front of you, palms facing the participants).

DEVELOPMENT I

Teacher To Students

"This time just this side of the room (half of the group) will play with me.... We'll call you Group One (play the marching rhythm while half the group claps).... Group One keeps on clapping while I change to another beat.... When you hear me change, Group Two (the other half of the group) does the new beat (there are two different movements going on at the same time).... Next time Group Two will start." (Keep a combination of two different beats going until you have exhausted all of the possible combinations.)

133

To The Teacher

You can split your group into threes and then fours, with three and four different rhythms occurring at the same time. If you are doing this game with a small enough group, you can use percussion or Orff instruments.

Hint

This activity is fun to use as a holiday game. Use appropriate words and sounds with the movement, such as "rattle, rattle, rattle, rattle," along with "owl, owl, owl, owl" for Halloween. (Suggested by Alice Corbeil.)

To The Music Teacher

A great benefit of Development I is that the children are hearing the relationship between the two rhythms. They can hear and feel how the two claps fit into the word *giant.* This awareness becomes a body knowledge that leads easily to an understanding of rhythm notation.

VARIATION

Use two different instruments, such as a drum and a tambourine. Play one rhythm on one instrument, and have half the group respond to that rhythm; then add another rhythm with the other instrument, and have the other half of the group respond to the second rhythm. For instance:

1. The drum plays the marching rhythm. The first half of the class claps. Play this rhythm for a few measures.

2. The drum continues to play its marching rhythm and the responding group continues to clap, while the tambourine plays the "twice as fast" rhythm and the second half of the group wags their heads. (If you use a tambourine, maraca, or bell, shake it to get the very fast "foot-tapping" rhythm.)

Hints

This is an excellent audience-participation game to begin a student-demonstration program. Your audience, both children and adults, becomes thoroughly involved and sympathetic. It is also a great game in emergency situations (see "Faulty Equipment," page 252).

Teachers who have been playing "Corner Game" from *The Art of Learning through Movement* by Anne and Paul Barlin will find this use of two instruments a valuable development. Two groups can be moving at the same time. For instance, one group can do "The Beach Ball" with the drum playing the "walking" rhythm while a second group is doing the "Spanking Run" with the tambourine playing the "running" rhythm.

Clapping Orchestra

For:
Ages 3–6 (A)
Rhythmic response
to music
Strengthening the
self-image
ESL

Teacher To Students

"Clap with me to the music....I'm the *orchestra leader.* When I clap, everyone else clap....When I turn my hand up, everyone stop....When I point to one of you, clap all by yourself....Now my hand says, 'Stop' to *you* and I point to someone else. ...Now it's *your* turn to clap all by yourself. ...I can also point to *two* people at the same time....My hand says, 'Stop' to you. ...And I clap to the music....That's right! ...When I clap, everyone else claps.... Who else would like to be orchestra leader?"

To The Teacher

The very young children seem to need frequent reminders to clap their hands when they want everyone to clap so the entire

YOUR

TURN

STOP

group gets to participate. When you are the orchestra leader, enjoy the music fully with clapping hands, bobbing head, and bouncing body. The children will catch your spirit. The power that the child orchestra leader feels when her/his peers respond to the "stop" and "point" gestures does wonders for the self-image.

Accompaniment: Side I, Band 1 (United States)

"YOU CAN POINT
TO TWO PEOPLE
AT THE SAME TIME"

Orchestra Leader

For:
Ages 3–10 (A)
Group rhythms
Body-rhythm
involvement
Self-image and
leadership
ESL

Teacher To Students:
Two Rhythm

"Who knows what an orchestra leader is?... Yes, and what does s/he tell the orchestra?... Yes, how fast to play.... How slow.... What else?... How loud and soft.... Which instruments should be playing.... And also, in what *rhythm** to play. ... The orchestra leader doesn't use words because that might disturb the sound of the music.... Let me show you how an orchestra leader might tell you, without words, how to play a two rhythm.... You clap."

To The Teacher:
Orchestra Leader Movements

1. Open arms wide to the side. "This means 'Get ready. Watch the leader.'"

2. Lift both arms overhead as you say, "And." Breathe in and lift your head. ("And" is sometimes called the "upbeat." The leader lifts for the "And" in the same tempo as for the following rhythm.)

3. As you say "One," bring both arms down to your thighs in a strong gesture.

4. As you say "Two," lift the arms and return them to the overhead position.

5. Repeat the gestures, counting aloud with the students until you feel that they have the rhythm in their bodies.

Down	Up
"One"	*"Two"*
Down	Up
"One"	*"Two"*

6. Warn them, "Watch me carefully" before you cross your hands for the "stop" gesture.

To The Teacher:
Orchestra Children

It seems necessary to have the children be a "clapping orchestra" before giving them real instruments. When they clap, they become used to making a sound with *each* beat. If they are holding a drumstick, they tend to imitate the orchestra leader and lift the stick on count "two," thereby sounding out only the "one" beat. Once you are fairly sure that they understand the need to make a sound on *each* beat, instruments can be used. If a particular child needs help, crouch behind the child, gently hold her/his wrist, and play the instrument along with her/him for a few measures.

To The Teacher:
Child Leader

When you say, "Doug, would you like to be the orchestra leader?" you will undoubtedly find that everyone wants that privilege.

To help Doug feel the rhythmic movements:

1. Stand behind Doug. Hold his arms gently by the wrists. Open his arms wide, saying to the orchestra, "This means that Doug wants your attention, so you will know when he is ready to begin."

2. As you say "And," gently lift his arms, extending them fully overhead. Let him feel the intake of your breath on the "upbeat."

3. As you say "One," bring his arms directly down to his thighs. Let him feel your increased energy for the "downbeat." (Modify the energy with which you make this gesture, according to the age and size of the child.)

4. Continue to help him until you can feel that his body has accepted the smoothness of the rhythm and that his gestures are large and clear. The largeness of his movements is important not only for clarity but also in creating a deep rhythmic experience throughout his body.

DEVELOPMENT I: THREE-RHYTHM MOVEMENTS

To The Teacher

1. "Get ready."... Arms out to the sides.

2. "And."... Arms overhead.

3. "One."... Arms strongly *down* to the thighs.

4. ''Two.''... Arms open out to the sides.

5. ''Three.''... Arms return overhead.

6. Repeat gestures, saying:

Down	Out	Up
''One''	*''Two''*	*''Three''*
Down	Out	Up
''One''	*''Two''*	*''Three''*

DEVELOPMENT II: FOUR-RHYTHM MOVEMENTS

To The Teacher

1. "Get ready."...Arms out to the sides.

2. "And."...Arms overhead.

3. "One."...Arms strongly *down* to the thighs.

4. "Two."...Arms cross in front of chest.

5. "Three."...Arms open out to the sides.

6. "Four."...Arms return overhead.

7. Repeat gestures, saying:

Down	Cross	Out	Up
"One"	*"Two"*	*"Three"*	*"Four"*
Down	Cross	Out	Up
"One"	*"Two"*	*"Three"*	*"Four"*

As the children become familiar with these movements, they will tend to get sloppy. Remind them of their responsibility to be clear and precise so the orchestra can follow them.

DEVELOPMENT III: TEMPO VARIATIONS

Teacher To Students

"This time we'll test you to see how well you are watching the orchestra leader. ... Bess, you be leader.... Bess will lead you in a two rhythm, but you won't know how fast or slow she wants you to play unless you are watching her arm movements.... Sometimes she will move them very slowly...sometimes very fast.... Sometimes she will just keep you playing evenly.... I wonder if she is going to surprise you.... Watch carefully."

DEVELOPMENT IV: MUSICAL QUALITIES

Teacher To Students

"Today we're going to play 'Orchestra Leader' in a brand new way. In fact, we have a very special visitor. Ely, come here.... This gentleman's name is Ely Legato.* He is a very famous orchestra leader who has flown in from San Francisco just to lead our orchestra.... The reason his last name is Legato is that he likes to lead his orchestra with very smooth and flowing movements. His arms never jerk or make sharp movements. They always flow."

To The Teacher

Stand behind "Ely," ask him what rhythm he wants to lead, then hold his wrists and direct his arms so they move smoothly and flowingly. Have the class repeat the word *legato* a number of times while they are doing this movement and feeling this quality.

The next "Orchestra Leader" child could be called Susan Staccato* for the sharp, abrupt movement quality. Other qualities that the children can learn are *forte*, which means strong and forceful, and *pizzicato*, meaning short and plucking.

Hint

It's fun for the children to have each new orchestra leader arrive from a different and strange place. Names like Oshkosh, Timbuktu, Kalamazoo, Cucamonga, and Chattanooga are favorites.

VARIATIONS

You can also name the orchestra leader after the gradations of tempo (rhythmic speed): allegro (fast), adagio (very slow), andante (walking), vivace (very, very fast), accelerando (gradually faster), and ritardando (gradually slower). They can also be named after the gradations of volume: crescendo (gradually louder) and descrescendo (gradually softer).

Meter

For:
Ages 6–10 (A)
Rhythm
ESL

Teacher To Students

"Can you all count to four?...Yes, of course you can....But can you count to four *listening to each other,* so that you say it exactly together?...I'll start you off with the word 'And,' then see if you can really stop when you reach 'four.'"

1. "And." (Children count together, "one, two, three, four," then stop on "four.")

2. "Good....This time, keep counting. After you say 'four,' start again with 'one' and keep going until I make the 'stop' signal."

3. "Good....When you all do it at the same time over and over again, listening to each other, you make a *rhythm.* What you were just counting is called a *four rhythm.* ...Do you think that you could listen to each other and make a *three rhythm?*"

4. "And." (Children count to three, repeating the three count until you make the "stop" gesture.)

5. "Good....Now it should be easy to do a *two rhythm.*"

Hint

In the *three rhythm* the children often pause after the third beat before continuing to the next measure. Remind them to say "one" immediately after "three," without a pause. (The pause inadvertently creates a silent fourth beat.)

To The Teacher

Once the concept of "listening to each other" is clear, instruments can be handed out to the children and the same problem can be explored. The children will often ask to do a five rhythm or a six rhythm. Any of these is possible, and all are fun.

DEVELOPMENT I: ACCENT

Teacher To Students

"I will play on the drum for you and you tell me whether I am playing a three rhythm or a four or a two or a five.... Listen....How did you know which one it was?...Yes, the strong beat is always count 'one.'...So every time you hear the 'one' you start to count again....Let's try this rhythm....What was that?...Good!... That strong beat has a name in music. It's called the *accent.** Every time I play the *accent,* you clap your hands....This time, instead of a hand clap, nod your head on each *accent.*...Let's stand up....I'll change the rhythm....On each *accent,* you do something with your arms....This time do something with your legs....This time with your back."

THE DRUM
OR MUSIC
ACTS AS
AN OUTSIDE
OBJECTIVE
AUTHORITY
SAYING,
"EVERYONE
STAY
TOGETHER."

To The Teacher

As the children move on the accents with various parts of their bodies, they develop a kinaesthetic response to the rhythmic measures and musical phrasing. When you feel that they understand what an accent is, do the exercise with music.

Accompaniment
Four rhythm: Side I, Band 1 (United States)
Three rhythm: Side I, Band 2 (Poland)

DEVELOPMENT II: MEASURES

To The Teacher

Review the first "Meter" activity, in which the children count a four rhythm while listening to one another.

Teacher To Students

"This time, everyone count to 'four' and then stop.... 'One, two, three, four.'... When you count to 'four' only one time you are counting a *measure*.... You are counting one measure of a four rhythm.... Can someone count *two* measures of a four rhythm?... 'One, two, three, four; one, two, three, four.'... Good!... Can someone count *three* measures of a four rhythm?"

To The Teacher

Once the concept is clear you can then go on to, "Who can count *four* measures of a two rhythm?" and "Who can count *two* measures of a three rhythm?"

DEVELOPMENT III: PASSING THE DRUM

Teacher To Students

(You have just played the music for Development I. The children have been counting aloud with the music and clapping on each accent.) "Everyone sit in a circle (stand inside the circle with a drum or tambourine).... Who will count *two* measures of that four rhythm we were just listening to?... Good, Josie.... I'll start with Josie (hold the drum so Josie can tap it with her hand).... Josie, while the music is playing and everyone is counting, you will tap *two* measures of a four rhythm on the drum. Steve, who is sitting next to you, will tap the next two measures. Mark will tap the next two, and so on.... I will move around the circle holding the drum for each of you to do *two* measures. The music and counting will keep going, so try not to miss a beat between people."

Accompaniment: Side I, Band 1

147

Swing Your Arms

For:
Ages 3–8
Identifying body parts
Singing and moving
Individual expression
Warm-up
ESL

To The Teacher

Move and sing. The children will move with you.

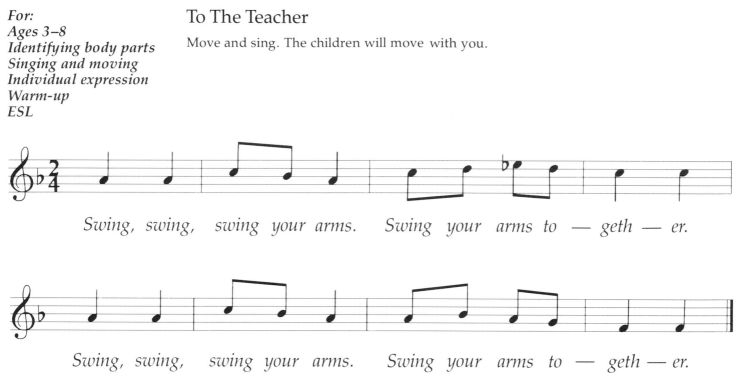

Swing, swing, swing your arms. Swing your arms to — geth — er.

Swing, swing, swing your arms. Swing your arms to — geth — er.

Teacher To Students

"What can we do with our legs?... Good!
    Slap, slap, slap your thighs
    Slap your thighs together.

"Can we move other parts?... Shoulders?
    Shrug, shrug, shrug your shoulders
    Shrug your shoulders together.

"What else can we do?"

To The Teacher

Other movements you can do to this music:
    Wiggle your toes
    Wriggle your nose
    Twinkle your fingers
    Blink your eyes
    Hop around
    Turn around
    Kick the air
    Reach up high
    Swing your hips

"SHAKE,

SHAKE,

SHAKE MY HANDS"

Cuckoo in the Woods

For:
Ages 3–10 (A)
Kinaesthetic response
to music
Concentration
Pantomime
ESL

Teacher To Students

''Everyone sit here and listen to this record.
. . . Listen for a special sound. . . . I won't
tell you what the sound is. . . . Listen carefully. . . . When you hear something strange,
lift your hand. . . . When the sound stops,
put your hand down.''

To The Teacher

The music alternates between a peaceful
walking rhythm and the delightful, playful
sound of the cuckoo bird. The phrase
lengths are uneven, so the cuckoo sounds
always turn up unexpectedly. One or two
children may tentatively lift a hand after
hearing the sound for the second time.
When they catch your approving eye, they
become more confident. Pretty soon, others
catch on and also lift their hands. Long
before the record is over, the entire class is
sure that they have isolated the right sound.

Teacher To Students

''Great! Everybody heard it. . . . What kind
of a sound was it? . . . A bird. . . . Yes, what
kind of bird? . . . Yes, it's called a cuckoo
because it sounds as though it's really saying 'cuckoo.' . . . Let's all get up. . . . Take
space. . . . Each one of you is in the woods,
all alone. . . . Walk to the music. . . . The air
smells delicious. . . . The trees are very

tall.... Pine trees.... Aspen trees.... Look at the tops of the trees.... You can hardly see the sky.... Suddenly, stop and listen. ...Turn your head.... You hear a cuckoo! ...Where is the sound coming from? ...You can't see the bird.... Walk again.... There it is again.... Stop.... Turn your head.... It flew to the other side.... The bird is teasing you.... It's so high up that you can't see it. You can only hear it.... Walk again.... Every time you hear the cuckoo sound, stop and turn your head to listen. When the sound stops and the walking music starts again, you walk again.... The bird keeps surprising you.... Every time you stop to listen, tilt your head in a different direction.''

Accompaniment

''Cuckoo in the Woods'' from the *Carnival of the Animals* by Saint-Saëns.

For additional ''Rhythm and Music'' activities, see:

151

Emotional Expression

Talking Rhythms

For:
Ages 4–9 (A)
Emotional expression
Warm-up
Improvisation
ESL

To The Teacher

You are playing a continuous beat on the drum or tambourine. The tempo is about that of a march. You continue the same rhythmic beat as you motivate the various movements.

Teacher To Students

"I wonder what we can do to this rhythm. . . . Let's start by clapping our hands. . . . Could we do something with our heads? . . . Look, Josh is saying yes with his head. . . . Let's all say yes. . . . Danny was saying no. . . . Let's all say no. . . . Can you say something with your shoulders? With your feet? . . . It looks like Rachel is saying, 'I'm *mad*!' with her feet. . . . Can we all say, 'I'm *mad*!'? . . . Can you be angry with your hands? . . . Sean is squeezing his hands and making a hard fist, punching the air. . . . Let's all try that. . . . Maya is giving each hand a turn to slap the floor. . . . Can you be angry with your whole body? . . . Michael is jumping up and down and making angry sounds (see 'Noise in the Classroom,' page 18). . . . Nellie is twisting hard from one side to the other."

To The Teacher

The children will be stimulated by the constant rhythmic beat and by your involvement. Because you are encouraging the children to express their individuality and because you are suggesting that the group do "Johnny's movement," the children learn that their unique contributions have value for the group.

DEVELOPMENT I: OTHER EMOTIONS

To The Teacher

Allow the previous approach to flow into the expression of other feelings. Say, "You can say other things with your feet. . . . How would you say, 'I'm shy' with your feet? . . . How would you say, 'I'm shy' with your shoulders? . . . See, your body can really talk! . . . Can your head say, 'I'm sad'? . . . Can your whole body say it? . . . Can your whole body say, 'I'm scared'? . . . 'I'm

happy'?...Let's move our whole bodies to some happy music!''

Other emotions include:

Shyness

Fear

Sadness

Joy

Anger

Peace

Accompaniment

In the beginning, your drumbeat will be sufficient.... Later, music can be added.

VARIATION: MUSIC INTERPRETATION

During a later lesson, reverse the process by playing the music for ''Moving Colors'' (Side IV, Bands 2 and 3). Have the children respond verbally and with body movements to the emotions they hear in the music.

Talking Bodies

While the teacher is focusing on what she is teaching, what else are the children learning?

The Snowball Fight

For:
Ages 4–10 (A)
Emotional release
Pantomime
Improvisation

Teacher To Students

"What do children like to do when there's lots of snow on the ground?... Sleigh ride?... Make snowmen?... and snow women?... Have snowball fights?... Would you like to have a pretend snowball fight? ...Okay.... If we make one rule, we can throw as hard as we like.... The rule is *no touching*.... If we *don't touch* each other no one will get hurt.... What do you do when someone throws a snowball at you? ...Don't forget to duck!... Start when the music starts.... Stop when the music stops."

To The Teacher

With this approach, you have created a safe environment in which the children can release some of their pent-up angry feelings. In the act of throwing a snowball, they are letting out potentially destructive impulses through a harmless game which becomes joyful and physically exhilarating. Informing the children to "stop when the music stops" allows them to be free within a controlled time span. You decide when to stop the music.

Hint

When you, the teacher, enter the game, the children have an opportunity to pretend to throw snowballs at you and you have the opportunity to return the compliment. Since this vigorous activity is done in a spirit of fun, it tends to break through previous barriers and to create feelings of trust.

DEVELOPMENT I: WITH SOUND

Add a heavy grunt to the throwing action. Adding the voice to the body action results in greater involvement.

Accompaniment: Side I, Band 4 (Mexico)

AGGRESSION

Children often find their own outlets. Pillow fights and water fights give harmless

expression to their aggressive feelings. Dance-movement class can also

provide a safe and socially acceptable environment for releasing aggression.

When a child hits another child with an *imaginary* snowball—when that

child is clearly aware that the action is a fantasy—

then the activity is healthy and positive.

161

Moving Colors

For:
Ages 6–12 (A)
Emotional expression
Interpretation of music
Intercultural awareness
Improvisation

Teacher To Students: Procedure

"Name some colors . . . red . . . blue . . . orange. (Allow the children to continue naming colors until they have exhausted their supply. If need be, stimulate them by suggesting "silver" or "rainbow.") . . . Do you think that different colors make you feel different? . . . If you walked into a room that was painted yellow, how would you feel? . . . If you walked into a room that was painted all dark purple, how would you feel? . . . People feel differently about colors, don't they? . . . To some people, gray is a very sad color. . . . To some people, gray is very soft and cozy and quiet. . . . Let's all stand up. . . . Show me with your bodies how yellow makes you feel. . . . Now show me how black makes you feel. . . . Now lavender."

To The Teacher

Before the children stand up to move, encourage them to describe their emotional response to the colors with "movement words." For instance: "happy and jumpy"; "sad and slow"; "frightened and jerky." These movement suggestions will help them to move more expressively.

Teacher To Students: Listening for Colors in Music

"Lie or sit on the floor with your eyes closed. . . . I'm going to play some music for you. . . . At the end of each section of music, I will stop the record. Tell me what colors you felt were in the music and what kinds of movements you might do."

To The Teacher

Just lift the needle off the record at any point, then replace it at some other point. The record for this exercise includes so great a variety of musical qualities that it makes little difference where you place the needle.

Communicate through your own enthusiasm that you find it interesting that "everyone has different feelings about colors and music."

DEVELOPMENT I: COLOR GAME

Teacher To Students

"Take space.... When you hear the music, you will move with whatever color feeling the music gives you.... When the music stops, you hold your last position.... Hold very still.... If one foot is up in the air, put the toe down on the floor, so you'll be able to hold your balance.... Catch your breath and lift your heels slightly off the ground, as though someone just surprised you.... When the next musical selection plays, you move with a different color feeling.... When it stops, hold still again."

Accompaniment: Side IV, Band 2

There are many different countries represented on this band. This is a wonderful vehicle for making children aware of the ethnic variety of musical expression. Allow the awareness of these differences to come from the children (see Development II).

Origin	Color Feeling
USSR	happy, festive
France	melancholy
Trinidad	fast and free
Greece	loving
Spain	angry, nervous
Mediterranean	shy, timid
Bali	confused

Germany	elegant
Israel	peaceful
Africa	exciting
Japan	quiet, thoughtful
Italy	delighted
East India	mysterious
Mexico	happy, festive

DEVELOPMENT II: "LET'S DO THE OPPOSITE"

Teacher To Students

(See "Do the Opposite," page 9.) "This time, we'll do just the opposite!... While the music is playing, hold still.... While you are holding, think about the color of the music; the way it makes you feel; and the kind of movements you would do to it.... Open your pores and let the color feeling flow into your bodies.... You know, you have pores on your skin all over your body.... They're like little holes that can let the color and music flow into you.... Feel how that music is making you feel as it flows into you.... Then, when the music stops, dance and let the music and color feelings flow out of you.... Could you hear different kinds of music?... What kinds?... Happy?... Sad?... Exciting?... Mysterious? ...Japanese?... Good, let's try again."

To The Teacher

If you enjoy moving with your children, join them. They will be inspired by your involvement. When you feel that they are moving freely on their own, gradually move out of the group.

Hint

While the last piece on this band (the happy piece from Mexico) is playing, I usually say to the children, "This time dance *with* the music. Dance with a partner if you like." It makes for a grande finale.

Accompaniment: Side IV, Band 3

The music on this band is essentially the same as on the previous band, with a slight change in timing. Less time is allowed for freezing and listening and more time is allowed for moving in the silences.

Here is the sequence. (For your information only. Don't share the sequence with your children. The element of surprise is essential to the game.)

Origin	Color Feeling
Italy	delighted
Africa	happy, festive
France	melancholy
Trinidad	exciting, fast
Israel	peaceful
Spain	angry, nervous
Japan	quiet, thoughtful
Germany	elegant
Mexico	happy

169

Original Choreography

Color Dances

Color Dances

To The Teacher

Approach this exercise when you are working with a group small enough so that each child can be given time for individual work. Be sure the group has had many experiences with: improvisation; emotional expression; dances that you have taught them; and "Moving Colors."

"Color Dances" bridge the gap between improvisation and choreography.

Teacher To Students

"Each one of you decide on a color feeling that you like best.... You're going to create your own solo dance.... Go to a place in the room that's all your own and try to move the way that color makes you feel.... Choose a color that makes you move the way you really like to move."

To The Teacher

Allow the students time to explore. You can save class time by suggesting the above as a homework assignment. Make the assignment immediately after the children have been doing color-feeling improvisations, so they carry the inspired feelings with them for overnight digestion.

Teacher To Students:
Discussion

"Let's sit together....One at a time, tell the group what color you have chosen; how that color makes you feel; and what kinds of movement your body does with that color feeling.

"Think about how you would like to *begin* your dance....What do you want the audience to see first when the curtain opens or when the lights are turned up?... You might want to start in a position on the stage....If so, decide what your opening position is and where you will first be seen.... You can be right in the middle; you can be in one corner; you can be away from the audience or close to the audience; you can be facing the audience or have your back to them....Choose an opening position only if you have decided to start on-stage....If you want to start offstage, find a movement for your entrance....Decide from which side you want to come.... Maybe you would like to enter from the back of the stage; from a corner close to the audience; or away from the audience.... If you have decided to start offstage, choose only an entrance movement....Take space and work on your own."

To The Teacher

By requesting that they create *only* one movement, you are relieving the fear of having to "create a whole dance." As the process continues, confidence grows.

173

Teacher To Students

"Let's all sit here and be the audience.... We'll watch Hilary's opening.... Hilary, what is your color?...Show us how you plan to begin your dance."

To The Teacher:
Constructive Criticism

From the beginning, an atmosphere can be established in which the child feels that you and the entire class are there to help rather than to judge. One of the best ways to guarantee this is to phrase your questions to the children in the audience so that they evoke positive responses. For instance: "You could really feel that she was expressing a bright-red feeling.... How could you tell that?...Didn't it make you happy to see her come twirling so swiftly onto the stage?...Did you like where she came from?" Gradually, being careful to emphasize the good points in the child's conception, you can begin to help her/him with constructive criticism. Ask the child in the audience who has a suggestion to demonstrate it. "Jonathan, you think she might come onto the stage from the audience?...You do it for us, so Hilary can see how that would look." The children all become participants in the choreographing process. Hilary's bright-red color dance will become the product of a group effort to which everyone has made some contribution. Hilary does not feel "all alone" with the responsibility of "creating a dance." At the same time, you assure her that she

can accept or reject any suggestion. "It's your dance.... You can do it any way you like." Each child is given equal time in this process.

To The Teacher:
Structure

At this point in the choreographing process, you have established the fact that every choreographed dance has a beginning. Your goal is to teach a very simple structural form: a beginning, a middle, and an end.

For:
Ages 7–12 (A)
Emotional expression
Music interpretation
Learning
*   to choreograph*

DEVELOPMENT I: CHOREOGRAPHING WITH MUSIC

The very first dance that a child choreographs should be quite short. (There are always exceptions, of course.) The beginning may be no more than an opening movement or position on stage.

To The Teacher:
Music

At this stage you might want to introduce music as an accompaniment to the child's dance. The choice of dancing to music or to silence (or to a poem or to sounds) should be left to the child. Eventually the child should have both experiences.

Teacher To Students:
Music

"Hilary, do you think that you would like to have music to go with your dance?...Is there any music that we play here in class that sounds like the happy bright-red feeling that your entrance movement has? ...The 'Leap' music?...The 'Jump' music?...The 'Twirling' music?...Let's try them and see if they fit your movement....Or maybe you have music at home that you would like to try out....Everyone, listen to your records at home and see if you can find music that feels the same way the beginning of your dance does. If you can, bring the record to class and we'll all listen."

Teacher To Students:
The Middle of the Dance

"Hilary, you have a beautiful twirling entrance....That's a good beginning....Now, what can you do for the *middle* of your dance?...If you want to keep twirling, maybe you could do it in another place on the stage....Maybe you could do it in place....With other arm movements?... Combine it with a leap?...Another step?... Maybe you can turn very slowly and still feel that wonderful bright-red color feeling inside you....Maybe you would like to do it on the floor?...Are there other movements besides twirling that give you that same bright-red color feeling?"

To The Teacher

The *middle* of the dance can be a very simple outgrowth of the opening movement or it can be quite sophisticated, depending on the individual child. If a child has chosen to do a two-color dance, the middle could be the second color or a contrasting color. If music is being used, the musical development may inspire the next movement. The above suggestions need only be made if the child needs your help. Allow the child freedom to develop the dance. The above ideas have come from watching what the children themselves produce.

Once again—as in all the stages of the growth of Hilary's dance—the children in the audience constructively participate in its development.

Teacher To Students:
The End of the Dance

"Hilary, you now have a wonderful *beginning* and *middle*. Your dance is almost finished. Begin to think about how you would like it to *end*. Do you want to continue the movement you are doing now and gradually slow it down until you are holding a final position?...Do you want it to end as excitingly as it began?...Do you want to be moving and exciting?...Do you want a sudden stop?...Do you want a surprise ending?"

To The Teacher

Children frequently assume that the *end* of a dance is a curtsy or bow. They must recognize that they should remain emotionally involved with the dramatic content of their dance until it is completed; that their bow is an acknowledgment of the audience's applause.

Teacher To Students:
The Bow

"If your dance has ended in a held position onstage, continue to hold that position until the lights are turned off or the curtain closes. If there are no lights, wait until the audience has begun to applaud, then slowly stand facing the audience, and bow your head. You are saying, 'Thank you' to the audience for their applause. . . . If you ended your dance with an exit movement, wait offstage for a few seconds then walk on, face the audience, and bow your head."

Accompaniment

Many pieces on the records express distinct color feelings and can be used for original dances. Try:

Side I, Bands 2,3,4
Side II, Bands 1,2,3
Side III, Bands 2,3,4
Side IV, Band 1

Response to Environment
Imaginary Props
Tree Shapes

Aesthetic Experiences

Response to Environment

For:
Ages 7–10 (A)
Stretching
   the imagination
Sensory awareness
Extending the
   kinaesthetic sense
Pantomime
Improvisation
Performing experience
Audience education
ESL

Teacher To Students:
Preparation for Walks on Surfaces

"What are you walking on when you walk to school?...Cement?...Grass?... What are we walking on here in this room? ...What is it made of?...What do you walk on at home?...Wood?...Tile?... Rugs?...What are some other things that people walk on?...Snow?...Ice?...As we are mentioning all of the different surfaces that we can walk on, try to imagine that you are barefoot and you are walking on whatever someone says....Pebbles?... Sand?...Hot sand?...Tar?...Good.... These are all things we walk on in real life....What could we walk on in our imaginations?...Clouds?...The moon?...Hot coals?...Bubble gum?...Feathers?... Whipped cream?"

To The Teacher

Get as many ideas as possible from the children. If they hesitate, suggest another surface. You will find that they are quickly stimulated into unlimited possibilities.

Teacher To Students

"Now we'll play a game....Let's sit on the floor in a big circle....Each child will get a turn to walk inside the circle and pretend to be barefoot on a surface....Then we'll guess what that surface was....You can choose something we've already mentioned or something new....Don't worry if someone else does the same surface you want to do, because I'm sure you will do it in your own way....If your walk is very slow, make a small circle so it doesn't take too long to get back....Everybody wait until the performer is back and sitting down before you try to guess the surface."

To The Teacher

In most guessing games, the children assume that it is the "guesser" who is being challenged. In this game we reverse that assumption by putting the responsibility on the "performer." A successful pantomime is one in which the performer is living the situation so completely that it is a compliment to her/him when the class guesses it easily.

Hints:

If no one in the class has been able to guess what the performer was attempting to express, ask the performer to whisper the surface in your ear. Help the child by suggesting additional action that will help

clarify the pantomime. If the child whispers, "I was walking on sand," you whisper back, "Try it again and this time dig your toes into the sand.... Wiggle them around. ...Feel the sand going between your toes. ...Or maybe you could make the sand very hot.... You have to pull your feet out quickly so they don't burn." In this way, you help the child toward a successful performance.

See "Audience Education," page 3.

VARIATION: ALL MOVE IN UNISON

To The Teacher

The entire class can move at the same time.

Teacher To Students

"Take space.... I'll call out a surface like 'snow.'... As soon as I say the word, everyone imagine that you are walking in the snow in your bare feet.... When I hit the drum or clap my hands, you freeze in any position and wait to hear what the next surface will be."

To The Teacher

It's fun to contrast the surfaces in order to motivate a dramatic change in sensory responses. Here is a list of possibilities:

Hot Sand	Straw
Ice	Water
Tacks	Peanut Butter
Mud	Cement
Wet Grass	Tile
Soft Earth	Snow
Whipped Cream	Pebbles
Dry Leaves	Tar
Worms	Clouds
Splintery Wood	Bubble Gum
Thick Carpet	Feathers

VARIATION: ATMOSPHERES

To The Teacher

Start by having the class sit on the floor in a large circle.

Teacher To Students

"Instead of feeling a surface with just our bare feet, we're going to try to feel an atmosphere all around us—with our whole body. Suppose it were raining outside.... Close your eyes and imagine yourself feeling the rain with every part of your body. ...Your face...the back of your neck... your chest...between your fingers.... How would your body feel on a cold day?

...Would it feel different on a very hot day?...How would you feel if you were walking through a strong wind?...How about a hurricane?...Can you mention other *atmospheres?*"

To The Teacher

Again, as with the "Walks on Surfaces," encourage the children to suggest a great variety of "Atmospheres." Suggest, "As each atmosphere is mentioned, imagine yourself trying to walk through it, feeling it on the bare skin of every part of your body." After the realistic atmospheres have been exhausted, suggest going into fantasy—for example, "walking through a rainbow." When there have been many atmospheres suggested verbally, repeat the guessing game used with "Walks on Surfaces." Give each child an opportunity to pantomime walking through an atmosphere, then have the class guess what that atmosphere was.

Now the entire class can move at the same time. After they "take space" you call an "atmosphere"; the children move and then freeze when you hit the drum.

When space is limited, half the class can perform for the other half. The waiting half is the "audience."

Suggested atmospheres include:

Rainstorm	Whipped Cream
Warm Sun	A Beehive
Hurricane	Under the Sea
Moon	An Avalanche of Falling Rocks
A Barrel of Honey	Soft Breeze
Snowstorm	Fog
Rainbow	A Barrel of Peanut Butter
Tornado	Jello

Imaginary Props

To The Teacher

You are sitting with the children around you. You are holding your drum or tambourine upside down, so that it simulates a bowl. Without talking, you begin to pantomime eating some grapes or cherries out of the "bowl." Take your time. Pick up one piece of fruit at a time. Pretend that an occasional one is sour. Handle the stems or pits as you would in reality. The children will be fascinated for a while. Stay with the activity as long as you feel you have their attention, then ask them the following questions.

Teacher To Students

"What was I pretending that my tambourine was?... A plate of cherries?... A bowl?... That's right.... It's really a tambourine, but I can pretend that it's something quite different.... And you can tell what that is if I do something else with it. Suppose I put the tambourine on my head, held my hands on it, and looked as though I were looking into a mirror?... What might the tambourine be?... Right, it could be a hat!... Suppose I wanted to imagine that this scarf is not really a scarf.... What else could it be?... A windowpane?... The sail on a boat?... An ocean wave?... Wings?... How about this chair?... Look around the room.... What do you see that could be a *prop*? A *prop* is something that people use when they are performing.... Choose any prop you like and imagine that it is something else.... Two or three people work together.... Decide what prop you're going to use and plan a pantomime that you will show us.... The class will then guess what you imagined your prop to be."

To The Teacher

Before the children perform their pantomimes, discuss what it means to be a good audience (see "Audience Education," page 3).

Tree Shapes

For:
Ages 4–12 (A)
Aesthetic awareness
Aesthetic relationships
Relating movement
   to sculpture
Improvisation
ESL

Teacher To Students:
Trees in the Forest

"Take space.... Let's be different kinds of trees.... Make a tree shape.... You can be a very tall tree.... You can be a small baby tree.... Every time I hit the drum, you change your tree shape.... If you are a wide tree, be a very narrow one.... Try twisting your branches.... Are you a very old tree, with lots and lots of leaves on it?... Are you a young tree, with just a few light branches?... Turn to face the sun."

To The Teacher

Make a new suggestion before each beat of your drum. Observe the children as they respond. Some children may not be moving freely enough. Motivate them with these suggestions:

"You are struck by lightning! One branch breaks off!"

"You are bent and twisted."

"Make your head part of the tree."

"You're a sad tree.... You're an angry tree.... You're a happy tree."

"Hold still.... On the next drumbeat, move only one leg.... Move only your head.... move only your back."

Accompaniment

There is no particular rhythm for this movement. Allow enough time between beats for each child to assume a position, but not so much time that the child is planning ahead. (See "Right and Left Hemispheres," page 25, and "Use Sound to Launch Movement," page 255.)

For:
Ages 6 and up

DEVELOPMENT I:
TREE SHAPES IN DUET

Teacher To Students

"Find a partner.... We'll make one tree out of two people.... One of you move on count 'one,' the other on count 'two.'... Decide who will move on 'one.'... You will have turns.... The rhythm is 'one and two and one and two.'... Move only on your own beat.... Partner Two, on 'two' design your branches with your partner's branches, so that you both belong to the same tree. ... Partner One, every time I say 'one,' make a new shape.... Don't move while your partner is moving."

Accompaniment

Play four measures of a two rhythm so that each child moves four times.

ANGRY
    TREE

To The Teacher:
Stimulating the Imagination

When the children have explored their own tree shapes for a few minutes, call on one couple at a time to perform for the rest of the group. The children who feel inhibited about moving freely become inspired and encouraged as they see the beauty of the others' sculptured shapes and hear your enthusiastic exclamations.

Suggest to the performing couples, "Hold your final position for a few seconds. ... Give your audience a chance to applaud." Holding a final pose becomes a way of affirming oneself—a way of saying, "I'm proud of what I have done." (See also "How to Encourage Variety in Movement," page 253.)

DEVELOPMENT II:
TREE SHAPES IN TRIO

Teacher To Students

"Divide into groups of three.... Take numbers from one to three.... One moves on count 'one.'... Two moves on count 'two.'... Three moves on count 'three.'...The rhythm is 'one and two and three and four.' On count four no one moves." (There are two purposes for the use of count four as a holding beat. The momentary hold gives the audience and the performers

an opportunity to appreciate the positions that the bodies have fallen into spontaneously. Moreover, the hold gives Child One a few seconds to assess the available space and decide where the next position can be.)

Accompaniment

Play four measures of the four rhythm.

Hint

The children will show a very strong tendency to move out of the way whenever Number One is ready to start a new sculptural shape. Remind them to hold their own positions while One finds a new place. The challenge to One's imagination is excellent.

To The Teacher
(of children ages 7 and up)

When and if you notice that your children's movements are small, tight, and self-conscious, use a fairly fast rhythmic tempo. When the children must move quickly and suddenly they are more apt to be spontaneous. When they take the time to "think," they inhibit themselves by prejudging their movements (see "Right and Left Hemispheres," page 25). Continue to motivate them to make large movements.

DEVELOPMENT III: WIND-BLOWN TREE SHAPES (LEGATO)

Teacher To Students

"Take space.... We'll go back to making tree shapes all by ourselves.... This time, instead of using a drum, I'm going to use a gong.... Imagine that you are a tree.... Hold a shape.... When I hit the gong, imagine that the wind is blowing you into a new shape.... When the sound stops, hold your shape.... When I hit the gong again, you flow into a new shape.... Each time the sound stops, you hold your shape.... Keep changing your shape smoothly, flowingly."

Accompaniment

Lyrical movements are encouraged by the use of instruments like the gong. Allow time for the children to flow into a new shape. Stop the sound by touching the instrument. Any instrument that carries overtones after being struck will work well for this exercise: a gong, a triangle, a drumstick hitting the top of a cymbal, an autoharp, or a guitar. There is no particular rhythm. Allow enough time between beats for each child to assume a position.

To The Teacher

The quality of these movements is equivalent to the musical term *legato,* meaning "smooth and flowing." Once the children have absorbed the new feeling, repeat Developments I and II in legato movements.

DEVELOPMENT IV: WIND AND LIGHTNING TREE SHAPES (DUETS)

Teacher To Students

"Find a partner.... One of you is the *wind-blown* part of the tree, the other is the part of the tree that is struck by *lightning.* The *wind-blown* part moves smoothly and flowingly; the *lightning* part moves sharply. You shape yourselves so that you are both part of the same tree.... The rhythm is g—o—n—g and *drum!* and g—o—n—g and *drum!* and g—o—n—g and *drum!*"

Accompaniment

You need two instruments for this exercise (a child can play one of them or simply hold it for you to play). One instrument is for the legato (smooth and flowing) sound, and one is for the staccato (sharp, cut-off) sound. The rhythm is a three rhythm, with the legato movement lasting for two beats. The staccato movement is done on the third beat.

To The Teacher: Further Developments

The combination of legato and staccato sculptural arrangements can also be done in trios. The legato movements are done first. To the sound of the gong, child "One" and child "Two" move simultaneously into a sculptural relationship. The staccato movement comes next. To the sound of the drum, child "Three" moves into a sculptural relationship with One and Two.

Hints:

In all of these partner and trio exercises, use "change to a new partner" every time you repeat the experience. Give the children as many opportunities as possible to learn to work with a variety of personalities.

A good motivation for the older children (particularly the boys) is to compare the legato quality with the "slow-motion replay" of the sports they see on television and in films.

VARIATIONS

Motivations like "Cloud Shapes" will stimulate other movement qualities and achieve similar aesthetic results. "Each of you is a drop of rain inside a cloud.... Get together with other drops of rain and make beautiful cloud shapes.... The cloud shapes can become mobile, and float smoothly through the sky, changing shape as the wind carries them."

Progressions

Progressions are movements in which you travel through space. All of you—the *whole person*—is involved in progressions. There is something extremely gratifying about propelling yourself through space.

Because a thorough warm-up is essential before doing progressions, it is best to do them at the end of a class session. They employ, extend, and bring to a culmination these elements:

A groundwork in *body techniques*
The ability to *align* and balance
A confidence in the use of *space*
A sense of *rhythm*
The ability to *relate to others*
The ability to *express emotions*

Backward progressions incorporate these additional values:

Taking a chance with the frightening unknown
Challenging the kinaesthetic sense, spatial awareness, peripheral vision, and visual perception
Building great body confidence

196

Preparation

For:
Avoiding discipline
  problems
Teaching children
  the value of observing
  one another
Making maximum use
  of available space
Providing the chance
  to watch the children
  individually

To The Teacher:
Floor Plan for Progressions

After the first person starts the progression, allow enough space between those moving on the diagonal for you to observe each child individually. As each child progresses, make comments that will be both helpful and encouraging. Suggest to the children observing in line, "Watch carefully and listen to what I say to each child. Choose the suggestion that feels right for you and use it when your turn comes."

In figure 1, the children are lined up along one wall. They are facing the center of the room, so that all of the children can see the individual who will be progressing through space. The child doing the progression always begins from the upper corner and progresses diagonally to the opposite corner. As each child takes a turn, the line gradually moves up towards the starting point.

1

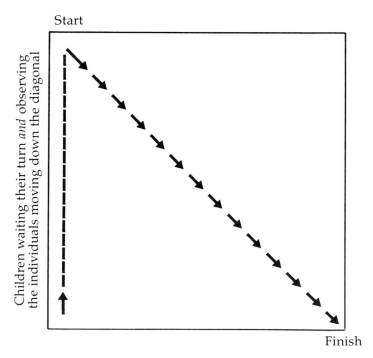

Start

Children waiting their turn *and* observing the individuals moving down the diagonal

Finish

198

As each child completes the progression, s/he stops and walks in turn to the New Start corner (figure 2). As they take their places along the new wall, the children once again turn to the center of the room to observe.

When *all* of the children have completed one progression, they are ready to begin again from the New Start position (figure 3). They will now travel on the opposite diagonal.

You will find it extremely helpful to establish this floor plan for progressions right from the start. The children will become accustomed to it and will accept it.

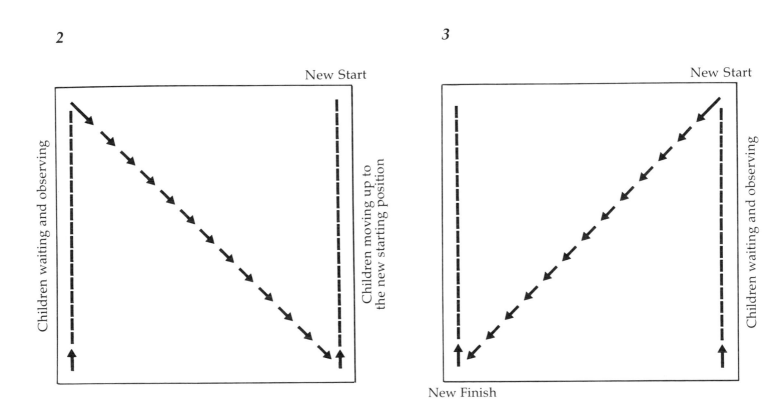

2

New Start

Children waiting and observing

Children moving up to the new starting position

3

New Start

Children waiting and observing

New Finish

To The Teacher:
Observer Attitude

By presenting positive alternatives to the usual boredom that ensues when children have to "wait in line," you will be able to avoid most of the problems that usually arise ("He pushed me," "She got in front of me"). Say, "Turn and watch Johnny while he is leaping. You may hear me say, 'Good, Johnny!' or you may hear me say, 'Spread your wings, Johnny!' and then you will know just what you have to remember to do when it's your turn." Also tell them, "You're luckiest when you're at the *end* of the line. That way you get to see many more people and hear all of the different things that I say to them. By the time it's your turn, you'll be able to do it *really* well." In this way, the children are involved visually and kinaesthetically and you are helping them to develop the habit of learning through observing.

Hints

One way to avoid always having the same child leading out is to suggest that s/he go to the end of the line after having a turn to lead. This sometimes creates a new problem, since some children prefer to be close to the front so they can lead, while others prefer to remain in the background. I find it best to arbitrarily call a name for each progression and ask that child to lead out. Sometimes I will choose a child who is outstanding in that particular skill; sometimes I choose one who needs to develop more confidence.

Sometimes there are chairs or benches along a wall where the students have to wait their turn to do a movement. If I see my students sit down when they need to be alertly observing others, I motivate them with the image of a sports hero. "Why is it bad for your muscles when you sit down during a movement class? Have you noticed on television programs that track runners continue to run after reaching the goal line? They gradually slow down to a walk, then finally stop. It's very important for your muscles that you do not stop too suddenly. It is especially bad if you are going to jump up and be very active again."

Slides

To The Teacher:
Preparation for Slides

Ask the children to slide across the room one at a time. Each of them faces you. When the entire class has crossed the room, they return individually. Again they are facing you, so that they are forced to start on the other foot. In this way, you have an opportunity to observe which of the children are having potential laterality problems. (For an additional explanation of slides, see *The Art of Learning through Movement* by Anne and Paul Barlin.)

To The Teacher:
Correcting a Laterality Problem

If the *right* foot is leading out and the *left* foot crosses in front of the *right* foot, this action indicates a possible fear of putting weight onto the *right* foot. (It could also indicate physical immaturity, in which case the problem may correct itself with time.) A simple solution is to ask the children, "Why do you think a slide is called a slide?" (Pique their curiosity by letting them give you their answers.)..."I think it is called a slide because you can hear it. Listen to the sound my foot makes when it slides to the other foot. You try it." Closing the *left* to the *right* foot while "listening for the sound" helps the child to experience the ability of the *right* foot to carry that weight.

DEVELOPMENT I: NAME-GAME SLIDES

To The Teacher

This game gives the children lots of practice in sliding with alternate legs. It also makes a great "getting acquainted" exercise for the first day of school, when you and the children are learning one another's names.

Teacher To Students

(The entire class is on the same side of the room, waiting their turns.) "Linda, when the music starts, you slide across the room all by yourself.... Your arms are open, wide apart.... You are facing front, looking at me.... When you get to the other side, slide back again to the class.... Keep facing front, looking at me.... When you get back to the line, take the next person's hand.... That's Pete.... Tell him your name.... Pete, you tell Linda your name, too.... *Both* of you go sliding across the room together.... You are *both* facing the front of the room, looking at me.... Linda and Pete, you are holding *one* hand.... The other hand is out at your side.... When you get to the other side of the room, Linda, you let go of Pete's hand and stay there, while Pete slides back by himself.... Pete, keep facing front, while you return to the line to pick up Frank, who's

A child involved through dramatic motivation bypasses the fear of putting weight onto the "unsure" foot.

next. . . . Pete, say your name. . . . Frank, say your name too. . . . Take each other's hands and both of you slide across the room, facing front. . . . This time, Pete, stay where you are. . . . Frank, return alone and get the next person in line.''

Accompaniment: Side I, Band 1 (United States)

(Suggest that all the children not sliding clap to the music.)

For:
Ages 4 and up
Variation for
   slide practice
Kinaesthetic
   relationship
   to partner

DEVELOPMENT II: MAGIC SLIDES

To The Teacher

Demonstrate with a child. Face each other, holding both hands. You are both stretching your arms as far out to the sides as is comfortable for the child.

Teacher To Students

''Michael and I are going to do a *magic slide* together. . . . Do you like magic? . . . Watch carefully, because we're going to make our feet go exactly together *without looking at them!* . . . We're going to look into each other's eyes. . . . You watch us and see if our feet are really moving together. . . . Did it happen? . . . You try it.''

To The Teacher

Have no fear—it will work! Look into your partner's eyes, smile, and you will feel each other's rhythm. It would be wise to choose for your demonstration a child who is not having any laterality problems and who

can easily coordinate in a slide movement.
   This variation of an individual slide movement is an excellent way to give the children additional practice in laterality coordination.

Hints

Have each child slide many times in each direction, so that both legs have the opportunity to lead out.

BOTH SIDES OF THE BODY

Whatever is done with one side
must be done with the other.
The brain records the total experience.

The partners' hands should not be clasped tightly. They should rest gently, one on the other.

Keeping the arms wide apart helps to expand the chest area. Looking into each other's eyes keeps the head lifted, so that the neck area is also expanded. This position evokes open, friendly, joyous feelings.

VARIATION: TWIN SCARVES

The partners face each other. Each is holding a scarf at adjacent corners. The challenge is "see your partner's eyes through your scarf, while your feet are sliding together."

Accompaniment: Side I, Band 1 (United States)

For:
Ages 6–12 (A)
Kinaesthetic awareness
Partner relationship

DEVELOPMENT III: "EYES IN THE BACK OF YOUR HEAD"

Teacher To Students

"Did you ever have a teacher who seemed to have eyes in the back of her head?... Let's see if Josh and I can do the *magic slides* back to back without holding hands.... Josh, turn your back to me.... Put some pretend eyes on the back of your head.... I'll turn my back to you and put some pretend eyes on the back of my head.... We'll open our arms.... When I say 'And,' we will do a *magic slide* across the room, back to back.... Really feel as though your eyes are looking into my eyes and the magic will make our feet slide together.... They will go exactly together, just the way they did when we were facing each other and looking into each other's real eyes."

To The Teacher

If in your demonstration you did not succeed in moving exactly with your partner, say to the children, "This takes a lot of practice. Children usually do it better than adults." Children are usually more "tuned in" to using all of their senses to detect what is happening in their environment. It may take a little practice, but they adore this challenge and will work at it enthusiastically.

Hint

Start each couple by standing between them. Touch the back of each of their heads as though "putting on the eyes." This contact gives them a tactile awareness that helps them to lift their heads and "tune in" to their partner. It also helps to avoid the temptation to turn the head and try to see with the real eyes. Start the children about three feet apart, since there will be a tendency for them to move closer as they slide across the room. If they get too close they might trip over each other's feet.

Accompaniment: Silence is best for this exercise.

For:
Ages 6–12 (A)
Rhythmic phrasing
Coordination
Joy

DEVELOPMENT IV:
FACE-TO-FACE
AND BACK-TO-BACK

Teacher To Students

''Take partners.... Julie and Tamara, face each other, look into each other's eyes. ... One arm points toward the window (any landmark).... We'll call that your 'open arm.'... The other hand holds your partner's hand.... We'll call that your 'holding hand.'... Take four slides toward the window while you look into your partner's eyes.... Then swing your 'holding hand' in front of you, making your body turn around so that you are back-to-back.... Continue in the same direction, sliding four slides toward the window.... Never let go of the 'holding hand.'... After four back-to-back slides, your 'holding hand' swings down behind your body, making you turn again to face each other.... Again you do four slides, face-to-face, toward the window.... Again the 'holding hand' swings in front of you and you do four slides back-to-back.... Slide with the rhythm of the music, repeating the movement with four slides face-to-face, then four slides back-to-back.''

To The Teacher

It is a help to the students to have them count out loud— *"one, two, three, four; one, two, three, four"*—as they move. Using their voices with their bodies internalizes the rhythm, helping them cue themselves for the turn.

Accompaniment: Side I, Band 1 (United States)

To The Teacher

When the children can do the above movement with some ease, challenge them by saying, "Now we'll do only *two* slides facing and *two* slides back-to-back. We'll say, 'Face-to-face and back-to-back; face-to-face and back-to-back' with the rhythm of the movement." The children use the same arm techniques. In this development, you are doing one and a half slides in order to hop and turn into the back-to-back position.

Accompaniment: Side I, Band 1 (United States)

DEVELOPMENT V: SLIDES IN A ROW

Teacher To Students

"Three of you stand one behind the other. Space yourselves evenly, a little more than arm's length apart. Bruce, you be third (behind Todd). Todd, second (behind Robert). Robert, first. Open your arms wide.... Get ready to slide across the room, keeping your line perfectly straight.

"Robert, be careful to go slowly, using the eyes in the back of your head to be sure that Todd and Bruce can stay with you. Todd, you are using your real eyes to help yourself stay with Robert, and the eyes in the back of your head to help yourself stay with Bruce. You also need both sets of eyes to help you stay in the middle of the space between Robert and Bruce. Bruce, you are using your real eyes to help you stay with both Todd and Robert. You also need your real eyes to keep Todd in the middle in case he moves too close to you, or too close to Robert. When they reach the other side of the room, three more of you line up.... Get ready to do 'Slides in a Row.' ...Start when I say 'And.' "

To The Teacher

Whenever this exercise is repeated, suggest that the children change their positions. Each child should have the opportunity to have the different responsibilities involved in having the lead, the center, and the end position.

Saying, "This exercise takes lots of concentration; you all have to be very quiet so you can tune in to each other," keeps the waiting children involved.

Saying, "Smile!" to the children who are sliding will release any tension that may result from their deep concentration.

Your class activity will flow continuously and smoothly if you give the responsibility to the children to be ready ahead of time. "As soon as three people have started across the room, three more of you arrange yourselves in a row.... Wait for me to say 'And' before you start." This expectation on your part will also help them to develop self-discipline.

For:
Ages 7–12 (A)
Spatial awareness
Kinaesthetic
*   awareness*
Group relationship

208

Expect the children to form straight lines with even spaces; don't let them expect you to physically place them.

Accompaniment: Silence

For:
Ages 8–12 (A)
Spatial awareness
Kinaesthetic
*   awareness*
Visual perception
Group relationship
Peripheral vision

DEVELOPMENT VI: TWO ROWS GOING THROUGH

To The Teacher

Line up three children on one side of the room. Line up four children on the other side of the room. All of the children are facing front.

Teacher To Students

"Keeping your rows straight and even, both rows move at the same time.... Slide across the room with the row of three passing through the row of four.... Keep your heads facing front.... Use your peripheral vision to pass through the exact center of your available space.... Stay in line with your own group.... Leaders, be careful to move slowly enough so that your entire line can stay with you.... Everyone else, use your real eyes and the eyes in the back of your heads to watch the spaces in front of and behind you. Keep yourself in the center of that space."

To The Teacher

This is a difficult spatial-awareness exercise. The children will need lots of encouragement. You will find yourself giving frequent reminders—"Stay with your group.... Don't rush ahead of your line.... The line needs to be even all the way across the room.... Wait for each other.... If someone moves forward or back, you have to adjust your spacing.... Look forward.

209

...Let's do it again.... It's getting better all the time." Suggest that they estimate in advance where their travel paths will lead them. They must establish their starting positions to make sure that they will pass through the exact center of the available space.

For:
Ages 8–12 (A)
Spatial awareness
Kinaesthetic
*   awareness*
Group relationship

Teacher To Students:
Returning Without Cue

"Set up your rows of three on one side and four on the other side of the room. You will again be sliding across the room and passing through each others' rows. But this time when you get to the other side of the room, you don't stay there. You return.... I will not cue you to come back.... Leaders, make sure that everyone in your row is with you before you return.... I'll say 'And' to start you off, and then you are on your own."

Accompaniment: Silence

For:
Ages 5–12 (A)
Group relationship
Rhythmic phrasing
Preparation for polka

DEVELOPMENT VII: CIRCLE SLIDES

Teacher To Students

"Hold hands while standing in a circle.... Make the circle small enough so that our arms can be low.... Our feet are apart so we can sway from one side to the other. ...Let's all lean in the same direction.... Bend your knee. (You lean to the right, bending your right knee. Wait for all of the children to catch on to the idea that the entire circle is leaning in the same direction.)...Now we'll all lean in the other direction.... Bend the other knee.... Change again, and this time we'll count out loud to eight.... *One—two—three —four—five—six—seven—eight;* (change sides) *one—two—three—four— five—six—seven—eight....* Now count four on each side: *one—two—three— four;* (change) *one—two—three—four.* ...Now count two: *one—two...* (change) *one—two...* (change) *one—two....* This time, instead of leaning, we'll slide.... Eight slides one way, eight the other.... Then four slides one way, four the other.... Then two one way, and two the other.... Repeat. ...Everyone count out loud."

To The Teacher

The final *one—two* (change) *one—two* movement is really a single slide with a step-hop in one direction and a single slide with a step-hop in the other direction. This is a polka step.

Just for fun, you might try a *one—* (change) *one—* (change) slide. It's a step that is commonly known as a "Soupy Sales." With one foot up in the air, you are sliding on your standing foot in the direction of the raised foot. That requires only one beat (count). The other foot comes down to the floor for the next beat, in time to repeat the same slide on the other side.

Accompaniment: Side I, Band 1 (United States)

When this exercise is first experienced, the children love counting the rhythm aloud with no music.

Skips

For:
Ages 4–10 (A)
Laterality
Confidence in leaving
the ground
Joy
ESL

To The Teacher

Children can develop very deep feelings of inadequacy when they discover that their peers can skip and they cannot. Sometimes these feelings can block an ability to learn. The skipping problem may be neurological or just one of slow maturation. The skip is basically a step and a hop on *each* leg. The child who is having difficulty is probably expressing a fear of leaving the ground with a particular leg. That child needs to be motivated to trust her/his weight on the "weaker" leg in order to succeed.

Ask the class to skip across the room, one at a time. Your purpose is to find the individuals who are having difficulty. If the entire class is skipping with fair competence, simply go to Development I. If one or more children are having difficulty, it is not necessary to point them out (they always know); just go into the following story for the entire class.

Teacher To Students

"I'll give you each a big round balloon from the magic basket. Whisper in my ear and tell me what color you want. . . . Pretend that it's a windy day. . . . Hold your balloon firmly, with both arms, so it won't blow away. . . . Don't pop it. . . . The wind is get-ting stronger. . . . Hold on. . . . Touch your knee up to the balloon. . . . The wind pulls you and the balloon up into the air! . . . It makes you hop. . . . Now touch the balloon with your *other* knee. . . . Again the wind pulls you and the balloon up and makes you hop on the other foot. . . . Change to the other knee and *hop*. . . . Change and *hop*. . . . You're skipping! . . . Knee, *hop*. . . . Knee, *hop*."

To The Teacher

Since you did not designate "right" or "left," the children will automatically start by standing on the leg on which they are comfortable. Some children will need special encouragement to "keep touching the balloon" and "*hop* up into the air" in order to trust themselves to leave the ground with the weaker leg.

Accompaniment: Side II, Band 1 (USSR)

For:
Ages 4–10 (A)
Laterality
Confidence in leaving
 the ground
Peripheral vision
Visual perception
Spatial awareness

DEVELOPMENT I: BACKWARD SKIPS

To The Teacher

Very often the child who is having the greatest difficulty with skipping can learn faster by trying it backwards. The natural fear we have about moving backwards helps us to balance and control our bodies in skipping backwards. We pull upward with the back muscles, balancing the lifted knee in front. The child feels, "I can take the time I need to hold my knee there while I try to hop on that weaker leg." It seems magical, but it works! Later you can say, "Steven, now that you can skip backwards, you can certainly skip forward! You just have to remember to keep that knee touching the balloon and let the wind blow you up."

Accompaniment: Side II, Band 1 (USSR)

The same music can be used in two ways. The children can skip to the music in *half time** (half as fast) while they are learning and need to take their time to "touch the balloon" before hopping. When they accomplish the technique, they can double the tempo.

Hint

For the child who needs special help, hold your own balloon while you face and mirror the child, traveling forward as s/he travels backwards.

Backward Walks

For:
Ages 4–12 (A)
Overcoming fear
Spatial awareness
Peripheral vision
Visual perception

Teacher To Students:
Backward Walks

"One at a time, come walking to me backwards. It's a game. . . . The rule is that you can't look behind you."

To The Teacher

Give the children lots of practice with movements that travel backwards. Overcoming the fear of moving into that unknown space develops a great deal of confidence. Help the child to trust that space by saying, "I'm here waiting for you. I'll catch you." As the others see that you hold and hug each child as s/he reaches you, they will accept the challenge. Also suggest, "Take long steps . . . reach each leg toward me," to help them learn to be adventurous and willing to explore.

Accompaniment: Side I, Band 1 (United States)

As confidence grows, suggest that they "walk with the music," stepping on each beat.

214

and Runs

DEVELOPMENT I: BACKWARD RUNS

Teacher To Students

"Run backwards as fast as you can.... Try not to look.... I'll keep talking to you so you'll know where to go.... When you get here, I'll catch you."

To The Teacher

For a while many of the children will "sneak" looks behind them. It's really very difficult to move freely into unknown space. Please be kind and patient. What they need is lots of practice. In time, you will be amazed at their courage.

Accompaniment
Walks: Side I, Band 1 (United States)
Runs: Side II, Band 2 (Italy)

TRAVELING
BACKWARDS

"Try not to look....
I'm here....
Listen to my voice....
I'll catch you."

Your reassurance
helps them conquer
the fear of moving
into the unknown.

Bounding Jumps

Teacher To Students:
Popping Corn

"What makes you bounce when you jump on your bed?... Right, the springs.... Pretend that this whole floor has springs under it.... Take space.... All at the same time, let's bounce like popping corn.... As soon as you hit the floor, bounce right off again.... Bounce from side to side... forward and back... turning around.... Sometimes your legs are straight in the air. ... Sometimes your knees bend up to your chest.... Some kernels can stay on the bottom and rest and then start popping again."

DEVELOPMENT I: IN PROGRESSION

Teacher To Students

"Come bouncing to me, one at a time.... Look at me.... Keep popping off the floor."

Accompaniment: Side I, Band 3 (Scotland)

DEVELOPMENT II: BACKWARD JUMPS

Teacher To Students

"Now that you all jump so well, let's play a game.... Let's see if you can jump *backwards*.... There's a rule to this game.... *You can't look behind you*.... Don't worry.... You will know where you are, because I will stand over here across the room, and I will keep talking to you.... Listen to my voice and just keep coming to me.... I'll catch you."

To The Teacher

Encourage with the tone of your voice, saying, "Great, Mary, you're doing it without looking!... Keep bouncing.... I'm over here.... I'll catch you." And when they get to you, they get a hug and a compliment on their success. As the observing children see the process and the relationship between you and the active child, they will lose their apprehension; in time, all will gain the confidence necessary to succeed. No one is put down for being tempted at first to "peek." "Try to do it without looking" is your attitude. Success will come if you believe in the child.

Accompaniment: Side I, Band 3 (Scotland)

DEVELOPMENT III: OPEN-AND-CLOSE JUMPS

To The Teacher

The children come across the room on the diagonal line, one at a time. They bounce continuously, alternating between closing their feet (first position*) and opening their feet (second position*) as they land on the floor. The same Open-and-Close Jumps can then be done backwards.

DEVELOPMENT IV: OPEN-AND-CLOSE JUMPS WITH PARTNERS

To The Teacher

Do "Open-and-Close Jumps" with partners. The partners are opening and closing their feet at the same time, while adjusting to the height of each other's jumps. Say, "Use your peripheral vision.* If your partner is bouncing lower than you, you have to lower your jump.... If your partner is bouncing higher than you, you have to push harder.... Go only as high as your partner can."

To The Teacher: Perfecting the Body Technique

It is wise in the early stages to focus on the spirit of jumping—the rebound off the floor, the fun, the challenge of bouncing with others. You will notice, however, the children's tendency to push forward with their stomachs as a way of trying to lift off the ground. This action results in arching the back and causes weak back muscles (lordosis*—see "Back Problems," page 4). I jokingly call this "belly pushing." I talk about streamlining the body—like streamlining cars. When the stomach pokes forward with each jump, the energy is dissipated in a forward-and-back action. When the body remains aligned, all the energy goes into the vertical action. The jump is higher and looks better. Energy is being used efficiently.

To The Teacher: Directions for Jumps

Watch for and suggest the following:

1. Lengthen your torso, placing your shoulders directly over your pelvis.

2. Push hard against the floor with your toes (resulting in a pointed toe).

3. Bend your knees as you land and push into a straightened knee as you rise.

4. Lift your eyes to eye level.

5. *Think up!*

Accompaniment: Side I, Band 3 (Scotland)

Gallops

For:
Ages 4–12 (A)
Confidence in
leaving the ground
Coordination
Laterality

To The Teacher

Begin by asking the children to gallop across the room one at a time in progression (see the floor plan for "Progressions," page 198). The gallop music, along with observing the other children, will help the child who is having difficulty. Make no comment until you have observed each member of the class.

If you do not criticize them, most of the children will pick up the catchy rhythm fairly well. After each child has had an opportunity to move across the room freely, you talk to the group.

Teacher To Students

"That was a lot of fun.... I wonder if we could gallop the way a horse really gallops. ... Maybe we could be a horse who is galloping in a parade.... The horse is very beautiful and very proud of itself....
In fact, we could be both the rider *and* the horse.... Pull your back up and sit very proudly in the saddle, holding your hands in front of you as though you were holding the reins.... When you gallop, bring *both* knees up in front of you, really high.... When you did it before, most of you kept one leg in front of the other, with the back leg sort of dragging.... A real horse will lift both knees high in the front.... Let's try it."

To The Teacher

In the attempt to bring both knees high off the floor, some children will deviate from the gallop in one of two ways: they will skip or they will run.

The solution to this is to begin by complimenting the children on their ability to solve the "high-knee" portion of the problem. Then say, "Did you notice that some of you didn't feel right with the music and the rhythm? That was because some of you were skipping and some of you were running.... For a gallop, *both* feet must be off the floor at the same time— as though you were riding a bicycle."

Accompaniment: Side II, Band 3 (United States)

For:
Ages 6–12 (A)
Coordination
Laterality
Visual perception
Peripheral vision

DEVELOPMENT I: BACKWARD GALLOP

To The Teacher

The backward gallop has the same advantages as the backward skip (see "Skips," page 212). The fear of moving backwards tends to pull the back up, balancing the body against the lifted legs. Remind the children:

1. "Your knees come high up in front of you."

2. "Try not to turn around to look....I'll keep talking to you....Listen to my voice. ...I'll catch you....Hold the reins."

Hint

Galloping sideways is also fun, although difficult.

Accompaniment: Side II, Band 3 (United States)

Twirling

For:
Ages 4–9 (A)
Spatial awareness
Teacher-student
  relationship
Right-left
  orientation
ESL

To The Teacher

It will help to have an assistant for this exercise. Any adult or older child who happens to be watching your class can help.

Teacher To Students

"You will go across the room one at a time, twirling around and around until you get to me (stand far enough from your group that they cannot see the color of your eyes). . . . When you get here, whisper in my ear and tell me what color my eyes are. . . . Keep it a secret."

To The Assistant

Stand behind the first child. Lift her/his arms to shoulder level. Stand so that the child is facing the front of the room, with her/his right arm pointing toward the teacher. Turn the child so that the right arm is going backward (behind the child). You don't have to walk around the child. Just stand in place and swing her/his arms around as though starting a spinning top. The child progresses, twirling, to the teacher. You remain in place. When the first child is approximately halfway to the teacher, start the next child.

To The Teacher

If the children are very small, kneel down so your eyes are on the child's eye level. Since most children are getting dizzy while coming to you—and possibly straying off the direct line to you—it helps to speak encouragingly. Say, "Here I am, Jay. . . . Look into my eyes. . . . I'm waiting for you." With your arms wide open ready to receive him, a smile on your face, and constant chatter, Jay will come to you happily. When he does, hold him; look into his eyes until he makes a guess at your eye color, then give him a big hug or kiss and send him to the end of the line. By that time his dizziness is gone.

It is important that the children experience turning in both directions. If you haven't the time in one session to have them repeat the turn on the left side, be sure to do it in a subsequent session.

Turning is probably the most complex of all of the basic movement skills. It requires intense body awareness while being uncertain of where one is in space. Choosing a point of focus ("spotting") is helpful. Of course, having you, the teacher, as the point of focus adds the human touch, making the child feel secure. It also gives you an opportunity to relate closely with each child.

There are children who will express reticence about being held or even touched (see "Touching," page 32). Sometimes I simply say, "That's all right. . . . Maybe next

CHILDREN LOVE BECOMING DIZZY

They seem to know that by twirling fast enough

the delightful experience of seeing the world turn around *them*

is something that *they* create.

They are playing a game with their kinaesthetic sense.

They are the center of their world.

time." Sometimes I make a teasing game of trying to catch the escapee. It all depends on your relationship with that child. In any case, the whole experience of: learning to turn; getting dizzy from twirling; having to see where you are (even if it playfully leads to the child's avoiding you); guessing the color of your eyes; whispering in your ear; being held by you; and the finale—getting a hug—is a delight for both you and the child.

DEVELOPMENT I: TWIRLING WITH SCARF

The child holds a scarf (shoulder level) in the hand that points to you. Saying "keep the scarf high" keeps the arms lifted while the child sees the scarf floating through the air.

Hints

Your assistant can help develop right-left awareness by saying to each child, "Your right hand is holding the scarf (and pointing toward the teacher). You are turning to the right when you make the scarf hand go behind you."

It is not recommended that these structured forms of twirling and half turns be substituted for the free twirling-to-get-dizzy experience, which young children dearly love. Allow separate time for the structured and the free experiences.

To The Ballet Teacher

Using your eyes as the children's point of focus is an effective way to begin to teach "spotting."*

Accompaniment: Side II, Band 2 (Italy)

For:
Ages 6–12 (A)
Spatial awareness
Right-left orientation

DEVELOPMENT II: HALF TURNS

To The Teacher

Be sure that the children have had experience with twirling before going on to half turns.

Teacher To Students:
Preparation

"I have an imaginary piece of chalk in my hand.... I'm going to draw an imaginary diagonal line from this corner all the way down the floor to the opposite corner. ...Can you picture that line on the floor? ...Good.... You will go down the line one at a time.

1. Place your feet comfortably apart on the imaginary chalk line.

2. Hold both arms out to the side, shoulder level.

3. Face so that your right hand is pointing toward me. I will be on the other end of the line.

4. Swing your body around, so that your right arm is pulling behind you as your left foot steps forward toward me (on the chalk line).... Keep looking at me.... You have just made a *half turn*."

To The Teacher:
Completing the Other Half Turn

5. "Your right arm continues to pull behind you.

6. Your head turns around to the right.

7. Your right leg comes around with your body and lands on the chalk line.... You have just made another half turn."

"Repeat the turn.... Keep coming toward me, stepping on that imaginary line every time you take a step.... Your right arm keeps pulling behind you.... Keep looking into my eyes the way you did for twirling.... Since the line is only in your imagination, you don't need to look down.... If you look at me, you'll be able to *feel* that diagonal line under your feet."

To The Teacher

You will find that at first the children tend to stop after each step, making the turn appear static and pedantic. When you feel that they understand the concept of stepping onto the imaginary line, suggest, "Swing your arms and head around a little sooner, to help you turn more smoothly. ... Enjoy it."

Hint

Be sure, as in all progressions, that the children also experience turning to the left. They are doing a left turn when the left arm is pulling behind them.

Accompaniment: Side II, Band 2 (Italy)

In order to move slowly enough, step only on the accents.

DEVELOPMENT III: HALF TURNS WITH SCARF

When the scarf is in the left hand and the left hand is "pulling behind you," you are turning to the left. Saying "keep the scarf off of the floor" helps to keep the arms up to shoulder level. (See "Twirling with Scarf," page 226.)

Accompaniment: Side II, Band 2 (Italy)

In order to move slowly enough, step only on the accents.

Listening Game

To The Teacher

Use the following culmination game *after* the children have become familiar with the backward walk, twirl, gallop, and skip, and with the music that accompanies them.

The class is divided into four groups, each representing one of the movements. It makes no difference how many children are in a group. Each group sits in a close unit as far from the other groups as space allows.

Teacher To Students

"*Walking* group, when you hear the walk music, get up and do the walk around the room. . . . Go wherever you find the largest space. . . . Don't separate from your group. . . . You can walk forward or backward or sideways or around yourself, as long as you stay with your group. . . . When you hear the music change, sit down as soon as you can, close to your own group. . . . The music will keep changing so that every group will have a turn to move, but you will never know whose music is coming next. . . . See how quickly you can hear your own music. . . . See how quickly you can sit when your music stops."

To The Teacher

At first you will have to remind the children, "Stay with your group." After a while they will become conscious of having to relate spatially to one another. The children who need to prove themselves by rushing ahead of the group will begin to accept responsibility to the group by staying with one another. The children who feel inadequate and are sure that they will not recognize their music become lost in the group and attach themselves to the natural leaders. Gradually their bodies feel the rhythm and they become comfortable and confident.

Hints

When repeating the game, assign children to different groups so they experience all of the movements.

The *skip* group can skip backwards or around themselves, the *gallop* group can gallop backwards or sideways, and the other groups can likewise vary their movements.

Accompaniment: Side II, Band 4

Backward Walks—same as Side I, Band 1
(United States)

Skips—same as Side II, Band 1
(USSR)

Twirling—same as side II, Band 2
(Italy)

Gallops—same as Side II, Band 3
(United States)

The first four melodies are in the above order. Subsequently, these same four melodies are played at random.

DEVELOPMENT I: OUTDOORS

To The Teacher

After it is introduced indoors, the "Listening Game" can easily be played outdoors. When music cannot be brought outdoors or when the outdoors is too noisy for sound to carry, use four cards in different colors. Each color will represent a different movement. Tell the children, "When I hold up the yellow card, it is the signal for the gallop group to gallop and when I hold up the blue card, it is the signal for the gallop group to quickly sit and for the skip group to move." The movement words can be lettered on each card (an aid to your reading program). With enough practice, the color of the card will become associated with the prescribed movement.

DEVELOPMENT II: TWO CARDS AT THE SAME TIME

Hold up one card. When the proper group responds, keep that card high and lift a second card. Two different movements are occurring simultaneously.

Somersaults

To The Teacher:
Preparation

Somersaults, like skips and cartwheels, are status movements children feel they must be able to do in order to measure up to their peers. Many children are frightened of somersaults because of past bad experiences. Be sure to use some kind of mat, rug, or even a thick towel. You need something soft that is as long as the child's body.

To The Teacher:
Procedure

1. The child is *standing* (not kneeling) at one end of the mat with feet apart.

2. Say, "Bend down and put the *back* of your head at the edge of the mat." Gently touch the child's head at the back of the neck. The child will naturally bend the knees in order to get low enough. The child's head will be very close to the legs.

3. With one of your hands tuck the child's head far enough under so that the back of the neck now touches the mat. With your other hand on the child's buttocks, you can easily flip the child over into a somersault.

The surprise and delight that the children feel when success comes so easily with no pain motivates them to try on their own. Caution them, "Tuck your head way under." Be sure that they always use a mat.

Accompaniment: Side II, Band 1 (USSR)

Cartwheels

To The Teacher

Announce that you are going to teach *cartwheels.* One child will probably respond, "I already know how," immediately accompanied by a demonstration. Since a cartwheel is a "status movement," the child often performs it with a "show-off" attitude, making the other children feel inadequate. I counteract this effect by saying, "That was good. . . . Can you do a cartwheel on the other side?" Most children who learn to do a cartwheel on their own learn it on only one side. It becomes very difficult for them to transpose this body knowledge to the other side. Working on that other side puts them on the same level as the children who have never been able to accomplish the movement. Everyone in class becomes a beginner.

Teacher To Students:
The Walking Cartwheel

"With your feet apart, stand on an imaginary straight line. . . . Stretch your arms overhead. . . . You are a wheel. . . . Your legs and arms are the spokes. . . . The wheel will roll, traveling on the straight line. . . . We'll learn it in slow motion first.

1. Put one hand (right hand) on the line. (The other hand is still overhead.)

2. Put the other hand (left hand) just past the first one on the same line. (The child's weight has completely shifted to the right foot.)

3. Put your foot (left foot) past the hand on the same straight line. (This is an awkward position, but it seems to be very helpful in the learning process.) Press hard against the floor. . . .

4. Pass the other foot (right foot) behind you, past the first foot onto the straight line. . . . Stand up. (The child is facing the same way as the starting position, ready to repeat the walking cartwheel on the same side.)

5. Learn the 'Walking Cartwheel' on the *left* side."

To The Teacher

After teaching the initial slow-motion cartwheel, allow the children to practice at their own pace. When you see that a child has achieved the correct succession of movements, help that child with the next development.

STATUS MOVEMENTS

Somersaults, skips, and cartwheels are movements that children feel they *must* be able to do to be accepted by their peers. Children who find these movements difficult develop deep feelings of inadequacy. Bolster their self-image by helping them to learn these movements early.

Teacher To Students:
Real Cartwheel

"This time when both hands are on the floor, instead of walking your foot onto the line, you will press your hands hard against the floor and *jump* the first foot onto the line. The second foot will come along by itself.... It also lands on the line.... Stand up.... You almost have it!... Now all you have to do is press your hands a little harder against the floor and lift your legs a little higher.... You're doing a real cartwheel.... Now let's practice on the other side."

To The Teacher

As the children become more and more confident with being upside down and using their hands to carry their weight, you gradually help them to improve their technique. "Stretch your legs long and point your toes up to the ceiling.... Straighten your knees and your elbows.... The more you point your toes, the longer your legs look." Be sure that the child is practicing on alternate sides. There is a great temptation to perfect one side and neglect the other.

Accompaniment: Side II, Band 1 (USSR)

Singing your name into the air coordinates
breath and movement. Using your voice with
your leap results in *total involvement*.

Leaps

For:
Ages 3–12 (A)
General coordination
Joy of vigorous
movement
Freedom to leave
the ground
Leg strength and
stretch
ESL

To The Teacher

Place a small soft object about halfway down the diagonal line (see the floor plan for "Progressions," page 198).

Teacher To Students:
The Gazelle

"You're a young *gazelle*....Have you ever seen a movie of gazelles in Africa?... They're beautiful animals with long slender necks and very strong legs....They run very fast with their heads very high in the air....When they get to a large rock or a huge bush, they push hard with their back legs, stretch their front legs, and *leap* very high over the rock....Pretend that you're running across a wide clearing.... You're trying to keep up with the rest of the herd....One at a time...open your arms wide...run...and *leap* over the rock."

To The Teacher

There is a wonderful feeling of confidence, expansion, and freedom when the children open their arms and chests and lengthen their necks.

Hints

When you notice a child really stretching both legs in the air, have that child demonstrate for the class. It will stimulate the others.

If you are using a drum, hit the drum *just before* the leap, to help life the child into the air.

VARIATION: LEAP WITH SCARF

The child holds two adjacent corners of a scarf. As the child stretches both arms high overhead and runs quickly, the scarf flies like a sail. Saying "reach up high and watch the scarf fly" is another motivation to extend the torso and lengthen the neck.

Accompaniment: Side I, Band 4 (Mexico)

For:
Ages 3–12 (A)
Self-acceptance
Self-identity
Use of breath
Total involvement

DEVELOPMENT I:
LEAP WITH NAME SHOUT

Teacher To Students

"As you leap over the rock, you will shout your name as loud as you can while you are *high* in the air.... spread your arms.... Make your neck long.... And say *Johnny* ... or *Sheila* ... or *Danny.*"

To The Teacher

The children who are waiting their turn become aware that you are giving approval to those who shout their names with complete freedom and abandon. It's gratifying to see the child whose voice could hardly be heard take courage from hearing other children shout with joy and exuberance. Here is an opportunity for children to use their voices at full range. The self-discipline is built into the exercise—"Shout your name only while you are *high* up in the air." It is unlikely that this will develop into uncontrollable "noise." (See "Noise in the Classroom," page 18.)

When the children prepare to shout before leaping, they automatically breathe in. As they shout, they expel their breath. Flow of breath enhances flow of movement.

Accompaniment: Side I, Band 4 (Mexico)

I pronounce myself
to the world.
I *am!*

DEVELOPMENT II:
LEAP WITH CHORUS

Teacher To Students

"Now the whole group has to shout the name of the person leaping over the rock. Be sure to wait until the leaper is *high* in the air so we all shout her/his name at the same time. Let's see if we know every-one's name."

To The Teacher

Here we have an added ingredient: the en-tire class shouts its acceptance of the indi-vidual child. The feeling that most children have as they soar into space hearing their names shouted by their entire peer group is one of extreme exuberance.

There are children who may find this complete acceptance a bit overwhelming at first. It may embarrass them. Very soon, however, they enter the others' joyful spirit and seem to be saying to themselves, "If everyone else accepts me, I must be okay!" If you have any class observers when you do this movement, ask them to join the shouting chorus.

Once again, there is no problem of "noise" because the group is reminded to shout only when the child is *high* in the air. The group remains organized and under control. What's more, the observers are thoroughly involved.

Accompaniment: Side I, Band 4

Once love for a movement has been instilled in a child, s/he can
work toward the far-away goal of greater technical perfection.

For:
Ages 4–12 (A)
Kinaesthetic
awareness
of partner
Spatial awareness

DEVELOPMENT III: LEAP WITH PARTNER

Teacher To Students

"Now two gazelles run and *leap* at the same time.... You each have your own rock.... Watch each other.... Spread your arms.... Run together.... And you *both* spring *up* in the air at the same moment."

To The Teacher

Two objects are now placed on parallel diagonal lines. Set them far enough apart so the children can run side by side, their arms fully extended from their sides at shoulder level.

The challenge is to run and leap "exactly with your partner." Although simply "fun" to the children, this development encourages a greater extension of the kinaesthetic sense. If space allows, this exercise can involve three children, then four—all running and leaping at the same time, on three or four parallel lines. Experiment with holding and not holding hands.

Accompaniment: Side I, Band 4

For:
Ages 4–12 (A)
Laterality

DEVELOPMENT IV: TWO GAZELLES, FOUR ROCKS

Teacher To Students

"This time each gazelle has *two* rocks. ... You have to run and then *leap...leap...* over each rock.... Leap first with one foot and then leap with the other.... You are still running and leaping exactly with each other."

To The Teacher

Place two objects on each diagonal line close enough that the child need not take any steps between the two leaps. The major value of this development is that the child is encouraged to leave the ground with *each* leg. "Both of the gazelle's back legs are very strong;...push hard off of *each* leg" motivates the children to exert equal energy on each side.

FURTHER DEVELOPMENTS

Further Developments of this movement include:

Leap over three rocks.

Do continuous leaps over a long series of imaginary puddles extending the length of the diagonal.

Combine partner leaps with name shouts.

To The Teacher:
Finale

"Leaps" is an all-time favorite for all age groups. The exhilaration that the children feel and the expressions of joy on their faces as they take that last leap and exit from class have never been surpassed by any other finale.

As each child does the final leap, s/he goes to locate her/his shoes. In this way, the children are exiting one at a time, avoiding the confusion that might result from their leaving all at once.

Accompaniment: Side I, Band 4

From "Rainy Day Dances"

"Hello, Rain"

Add choreographed dances to your dance-movement program. They balance the children's total experience. When a dance is designed for their age and experience level; when the form and structure of the dance are simple enough for them, but also interesting and challenging; and when sufficient freedom is allowed for individual expression, the experience will be an enriching one. Not only will the children get much joy from performing the dance, they will unconsciously learn about structure and form and eventually relate this knowledge to their own choreography and to other art forms.

If, in addition, the dance is done to a song, and if the

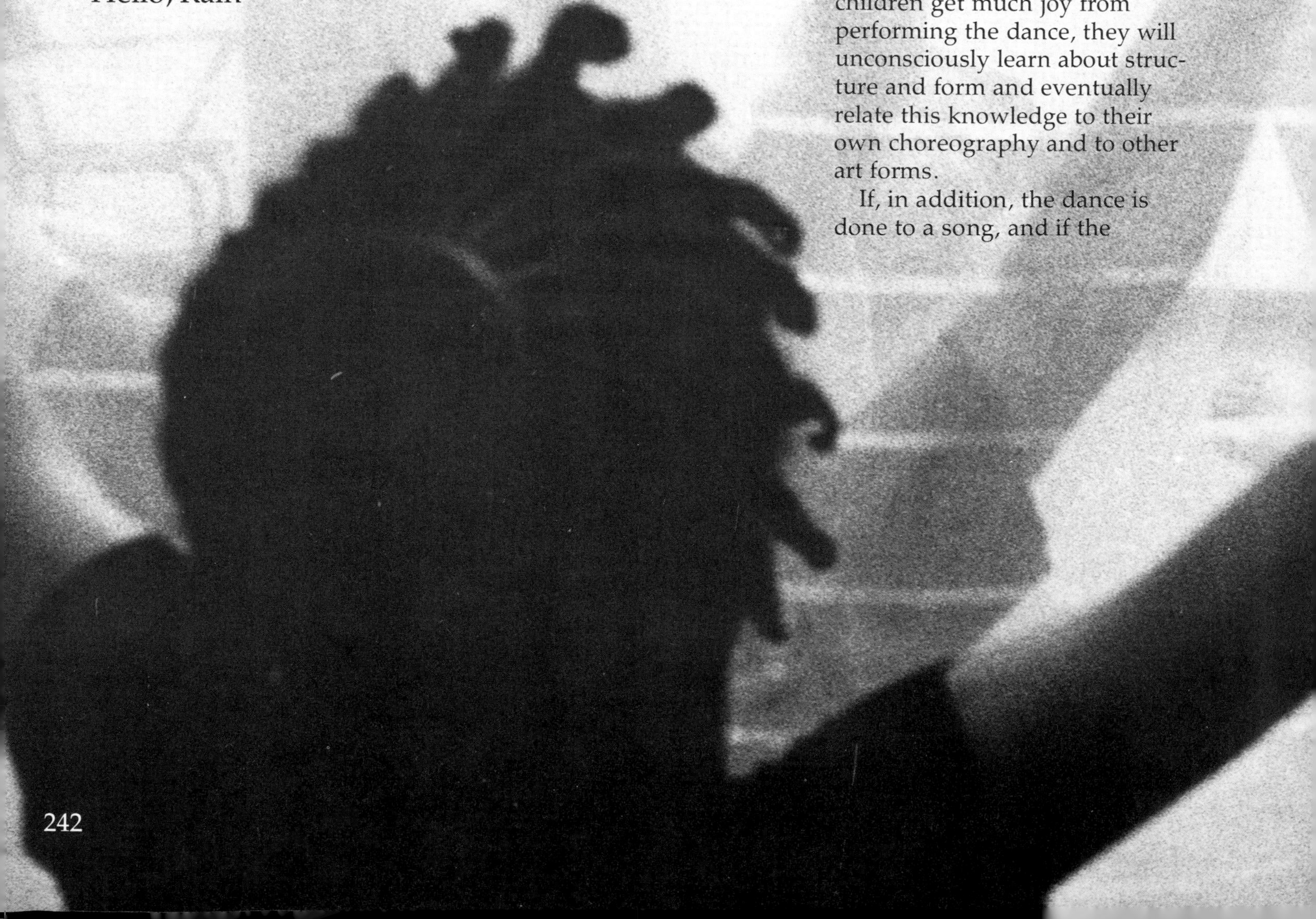

242

children can learn the song and be encouraged to sing while they dance, they are involving their *total* selves. The song used for the choreographed dance in this section is from the album *Rainy Day Dances, Rainy Day Songs* by Patty Zeitlin and Marcia Berman with Anne Lief Barlin.

"Hello, Rain"

(Words and music by Marcia Berman
Choreography by Anne Lief Barlin)

For:
Ages 3–10
Learning a
   finished dance
Experiencing
   a structured form
Joy
ESL

To The Teacher:
Preparation

The entire dance is done in unison. Everyone moves all of the time. The children
are each holding a corner of a scarf in
one hand. As you say, "This scarf is a raindrop...it just came down from the sky,"
you toss the scarf up into the air. If the
children are under six, don't release it.
Just float it into the air and bring your arm
down, letting the scarf touch the ground.
Continuing to touch the ground with the
scarf, you then scootch* yourself backwards, saying, "The raindrop is rolling
down a hill." As the children imitate your
movements, they will find that they have
made a big circle. I find this the best way to
introduce the first movement of the dance
and get the children into a circle formation.
The children sing and dance the entire
song twice. On the third repetition they
proceed up to the point just before
"Raindrops fall" (marked *fine* in the
music), and then end the activity by repeating the "Hello rain, hello rain" phrase
three times.

244

It's rain-ing to-day, It's rain-ing to-day. Hel-lo rain, Hel-lo,

rain. We want to play out-side to-day, We want to play out-side. Hel-lo

fine ⊕

rain, Hel-lo rain. Rain-drops fall, rain-drops fall-ing down, ev'-ry-

where, All a—round me. Rain-drops fall, Rain-drops fall-ing down, ev'-ry-

at second repeat:
da capo al fine ⊕ *coda*

1   2

where, All a—round. It's rain, Hel-lo rain, Hel-lo rain. Hel-lo, rain.

1

It's raining today

Figure 1:
A gentle run toward the center of the circle. The scarf is lifted gradually and tossed upward on "today."

2

It's raining today

Hello, rain

Hello, rain

Figure 2:
Bring the arm down so that the scarf touches the ground. Keep it on the ground as you each scootch backward to make a large circle.

Repeat figure 1

Repeat figure 2

3

We want to play outside today, we want to play outside

Hello, rain

Hello, rain

Figure 3:
(''You're very sad.'') In place, with your feet apart, you sway and wave the scarf from side to side. Keep the scarf touching the ground. (If you move slowly with the musical phrase, there will be four sways.)

Repeat figure 1

Repeat figure 2

4

Raindrops fall, raindrops falling down everywhere, all around me. Raindrops fall, raindrops falling down everywhere, all around.

Figure 4:

Everyone moves freely all over the room. The scarf is tossed up into the air and released, and caught as it floats down. "Sing and dance with the music. Your body also feels like the scarf, floating through space."

Wherever they are, the children come in toward the center and repeat the dance.

After the children have danced and sung the song twice and proceeded through the third repetition up to "Raindrops fall" (marked *fine* on the music, and shown in figure 4), they finish the dance with three repetitions of "Hello rain, hello rain" (figures 1 and 2). On the third repetition, the scarves are tossed high in the center of the circle (figure 5). Then everyone opens both arms and scoots backwards into a large circle *without the scarves*. The scarves are floating down to the ground as the dance ends. (If you use the record instead of the printed music, repeat the final movement four times instead of three.)

VARIATION

New words can be substituted on days when it isn't raining:

Hello, sun...sunbeams fall
Hello, snow...snowflakes fall
Hello, wind...leaves fall
Hello, clouds...clouds float

Children can use a "Hello, storm" lyric to express their fear of thunder or lightning by substituting "lightning strikes" or "thunder booms" along with "I'm scared to go outside today" at the appropriate places in the song.

Accompaniment

Rainy Day Dances, Rainy Day Songs (recorded on Educational Activities, Incorporated by Patty Zeitlin and Marcia Berman with Anne Lief Barlin) makes an excellent accompaniment for the dance in performance.

250

5

General Hints

Breathing

Tension in the entire body can be released by slowly letting out the breath. Focusing on a particular part of the body while exhaling has remarkable results. Most people forget to continue breathing during an exercise. Remind the children often to become aware of their breathing. Experiment with conscious rhythmic breathing.

Chewing Gum

Chewing gum makes your mouth move in a different rhythm from the rest of your body. It creates disharmony. It confuses and distracts the child and the teacher. *Anything* in your mouth while you are moving vigorously is dangerous.

Class Costume

When you have a regular day for your dance-movement sessions, remind the children in advance to wear clothing in which they can move comfortably. Tights or shorts under their skirts work well for girls; pants that are not too tight and a simple T-shirt work well for the boys. Pants or tights on the legs make it easier to slide on most uncarpeted floors. Bare skin tends to stick to floor surfaces.

Bare feet allow for the greatest freedom of foot action and foot articulation. Bare feet also carry an unconscious connotation of freedom, since they're associated with walking on the beach, on wet grass, and in puddles. Many children resist removing their shoes and socks in a public school because the indoor, regulated environment holds them back. Shoes can be confining, preventing the foot from exercising and growing normally. Many orthopedists are now recommending walking barefoot on the earth for a few hours each day to maintain foot health.

Socks should be removed. They are dangerously slippery on most floors. Tights that have seams under the feet can be opened about three inches at the arch, so the bare foot can be slipped out for dance-movement class and then returned for wearing the tights with shoes.

Long, loose hair needs to be tied back. When the hair is loose, children tend to make unconscious hand gestures to uncover the face and eyes, interfering with their involvement. Also, they need to become aware that these hand movements are seen by others and interpreted as part of their conscious movement. Loose jewelry and loose change should also be removed, for the sake of safety and to avoid distractions during class.

Faulty Equipment

No matter how many hours we spend in preparation, no matter how many problems our experience has taught us to anticipate—we always manage to run into trouble with machinery. An extreme example is having five hundred children anxiously awaiting a movie on a projector that refuses to cooperate. One solution: save the day by jumping onto the stage with your trusty drum and saying, "While we're waiting, let's play a game!" "Rhythm Game in Seats" (page 133) is ideal for such occasions.

Flexible Groupings

When you are creating a dance or setting a technique study for performance, be flexible to avoid absentee problems. Arrange your groupings so that it won't matter how many children are in each group (see "Listening Game," page 227), or who is whose partner (see "The Boy-Girl Problem," page 5).

Focus

When you would like a child to involve the *head* as part of the total movement, try, "Ben, look at the door with each swing." Choosing a point of focus for the eyes will correctly position the head.

Functional Movement

Use only the parts of the body that you really need in order to do a movement. When your children are doing an exercise that requires tension in only the leg muscles, observe them carefully. Are they tensing their necks, their fingers, their mouths? "Lengthen your neck" will relax the shoulders. Saying, "Smile" will do wonders to relax the mouth.

Giggling

Giggling can be a problem because it is infectious. Try asking, "Do you know *why* you're giggling?" The children may recognize the cause and feel sobered as they say, "I guess I'm self-conscious." My response is "I know that it's not comfortable to feel self-conscious." Sympathizing with the uncomfortable feeling that evokes defensive giggling and then suggesting a positive alternative results in gratitude and response from most children. For instance, in "Invisible Strings" I might say, "Sometimes those tiny movements feel silly and make you giggle.... Make your movements larger.... Use your whole arm.... Try to feel that it is your partner's arm that you are moving." Pretty soon your suggestions can steer the children's attention from self-conscious giggling to the goals of the movement experience.

How to Encourage Variety in Movement

Say, "Hold your body still and move just one leg...just your head...just one arm." (Try this with "Tree Shapes" or "Moving Colors.")

Change levels.

Change direction.

Change your rhythm.

Change your tempo.

Make the movement travel.

Master Your Body

When a child says something like, "But my arm doesn't want to stay there!" I say, "It's *your* arm. Just tell it what *you* want it to do. You're the master of your own body."

Microphone

Children love talking into a "mike." They can be called upon to put out their best efforts when they are given the responsibility of performing with a microphone. Try using a slightly older group of children to sing the song on the "mike" while the younger group is dancing.

Motivating with Language

When you are not teaching by demonstrating, the language you use must be relevant. Your language must motivate the children and clarify the goal of the movement. "Keep your arms out to the sides" creates a static response compared with "Reach your arms way out." "Stand up straight" is static compared with "Pull your back up tall. Make your neck very long."

No Space

When you have only enough space for a portion of the class, involve the remainder as an audience. Give the observers a *specific* problem to solve. For instance:

They could accompany the children who are moving with hand clapping, instruments, or rhythmic voice sounds or singing.

If they are observing a body technique like "Leaps" suggest, "Watch how wide their legs stretch. Count how many leaps it takes to get across the room."

If they are watching an aesthetic experience like "Moving Colors," suggest, "Later I'll ask you to tell me how many different feelings you saw," or "Which child did which feeling?"

You can suggest something quite arbitrary. For "Tree Shapes" you could suggest, "Count the number of levels the trees used."

The result of this involvement will be that the observers remain disciplined.

Another solution was found by a teacher with an open classroom. In the corner where she keeps the record player she put the records and the dance-activity books. She finds that an individual child will look at the books, play the records, and spontaneously move within the limited space.

If you have the use of outdoor space, prepare the class indoors. In the classroom, demonstrate specific exercises with a small group. You will find it much easier to communicate outdoors when the children have already internalized your goals.

Props

Keep props on hand that will stimulate the children's imaginations: scarves, ribbons, hats (children love to contribute). Bits and pieces of "dress up" open the child's world to magical hours. Just saying, "What does Dilim look like?" when she has donned that full colorful skirt can stimulate the creation of a full day's festival. Have a variety of records handy, so that you can quickly accompany any suggested mood.

Records

Allow yourself plenty of time to check over records, record player, cassettes, and other equipment. Have a drum or tambourine available for emergencies.

When you want to stop a record suddenly, cut the volume all the way down; you can then take your time removing the needle, and so avoid scratching the record.

Repetition

A physical skill cannot be achieved through intellectual understanding alone. A particular kind of coordination—especially if the skill is new or strange—or a correction cannot be learned by accomplishing it once or twice. Constant repetition is the only way to really learn a motor skill.

Shapes and Environment

Our physical environment has a strong effect on our kinaesthetic sense. Have you ever tried forming a really round circle in a long, narrow room? Inevitably, the circle becomes an oval. Low lights, mute colors, and an everything-in-its-place look cause voices to be quiet and movement to be slow. Bright lights, bright colors, and many objects scattered about the room stimulate sound and activity.

Children are even more sensitive to their environments than adults are. Experiment with changing the children's environment from time to time. The child who lives in an aesthetic environment will seek beauty in the world.

Stiff Muscles (as a Result of Work)

A good way to get over your aching muscles from yesterday's class is to work the same muscles today.

Straight Lines

It isn't always necessary to stand in rigid lines. It becomes boring to see nothing but the back of someone's head.

If the children must walk in an organized fashion from one room to another, experiment with alternate forms. Walk in rhythm; decide on an appropriate step, such as a skip or a slide; or have the group chant or sing an appropriate rhythm that will keep them interested and involved. If quiet is essential, a rhythmic whisper can be great fun.

Strokes

We all need approval and acceptance. Express yours with enthusiasm. When a child has achieved something after much struggle, say, "Wow! That's *great*! You really have it now." When visitors are observing, say, "Aren't they amazing?" To the child who is left out: "I'd *love* to be your partner." The "perfectionist" child who is constantly berating herself/ himself needs your strokes.

Take Space

During any exercise in which the whole class is working individually, the children will often tend to bunch up into small areas. Suggest, "Susan, would you go into that big empty space behind you?"

Use Sound to Launch Movement

If you are accompanying the children with a drumbeat for leaps, jumps, or any movements that spring off the ground, hit the drum just before a child is about to leave the floor. Anticipate the spring. When you do this, the children feel as though the beat of the drum is sending them into space. The gong with its overtones is an excellent instrument for leaps. Experiment with different kinds of drums and with a variety of instruments to motivate different movement qualities.

Glossary

Definitions given here are relevant to the material, methods, and philosophy expressed in the book. Dictionary definitions were included when they seemed useful.

Abdominal Muscles (Stomach Muscles). Dictionary definition: The muscle in the part of the body situated between the diaphragm and the pelvis and containing the stomach, intestines, etc.; also, belly.

Press the fingers of both hands against your belly button (navel). In a sitting position, lift both legs in front of you. You can feel the abdominals tightening.

Accent. The emphasis or stress on a specific count or beat. In classical music, it is most often the first beat of a measure. The word is synonymous with *downbeat* because of the strong downward gesture of the orchestra leader. An accent can be made with a sound (drum, voice) or with the body (head, knees).

Achilles' Tendon. Dictionary definition: The cord of tough fibrous tissue connecting the back of the heel to the calf muscle of the leg.

The greater the stretch in the Achilles' tendon, the more spring one has for jumps. Achilles was a Greek hero in Homer's *Iliad.* During the Trojan war he killed Hector and was in turn killed by Paris with an arrow that struck his only vulnerable spot—his heel. "Achilles' heel" has come to mean the small, susceptible spot which reveals mortal weakness.

And. In music the word *and* is a rhythmic preparation. It is synonymous with the word *upbeat.* The speed (or tempo) with which the word is said or gestured anticipates and establishes the tempo of the coming rhythm.

Arm and Body Successions. A movement succession implies an impulse of energy that releases a flow of movement from one part of the body to another. You can see the energy traveling in a smooth and logical sequence. Successions are closely associated with the movement style of Doris Humphrey, one of the originators of modern dance in the United States.

Atmosphere. All of the air in any given place or environment that pervades or surrounds you.

Barre. In dance studios: the long round dowel usually placed about three feet six inches from the floor and attached to the wall. Its major function is to balance the body by providing a place to rest a hand. It can also be used for leg stretches, right and left orientation, and spatial awareness. In the public-school classroom barre substitutes include the back of a chair, a stage, a table, or anything with sufficient stability and correct height (slightly lower than shoulder level).

Body Techniques. Dictionary definition of *technique:* The degree of skill or command of fundamentals exhibited in the performance of any task.

Body techniques are the physical craft of the art form of dance. See the introduction to "Body Techniques," page 36.

Buttock. Dictionary definition: Either of two rounded parts of the rump.

Centering. Dictionary definition of *center:* To concentrate at a center; to determine the center of.

In addition, *centering* implies an awareness through the body of the center of gravity. Aligning the body as you extend and lengthen the torso makes you aware of the point in the center of the earth which keeps you stable, grounded, and in perfect balance. (See "Body Alignment," page 83.)

Choreography. The art of creating a dance. A choreographed dance has structure and form. Its movements and designs are established in time and space. It has a purpose.

As opposed to an *improvisation,* * the movements of a choreographed dance are clearly enough set that they can be rehearsed, learned, and repeated. It is valuable for children to learn dances that have been choreographed by others, as well as learning to choreograph their own. (See the Introduction to "From 'Rainy Day Dances,'" page 242, and the "Color Dances," page 172.) When young children begin to choreograph, allow some improvisation. Adhering rigidly to the choreographed form can be too inhibiting.

Contrast. Dictionary definition: To set in opposition in order to show or emphasize differences. To show differences when compared.

A dramatic device used to point up extreme differences in movement qualities —sizes, shapes, or feelings. Sadness is more clearly defined next to extreme joy; straight lines are visually clearer next to circles and spirals. A device for opening up and reaching toward our fullest capacities.

Double Time. Making a basic beat or rhythm twice as fast—as used in music and dance.

Downbeat. A musical term which describes the downward gesture of an orchestra leader; designating the first beat of a measure; frequently the accent. The opposite of *upbeat.*

Downstage. Dictionary definition: Relating to the front half of the stage.

A theatrical term which stems from the days when stages were tilted and the audience areas were level. Actors standing closest to the audience were "down stage."

256

Exit. A theatrical term used as both noun and verb. The *exit* is the place from which the performer leaves the stage; *to exit* is to leave the stage.

Extend. Dictionary definition: To open or straighten out to full length; to unbend; to stretch out or spread to fullest length.

To reach out with muscles, ligaments, and imagination; to stretch through space beyond physical probabilities.

Eurythmics. A system created by Émile Jaques-Dalcroze early in this century, designed to teach music and rhythm through movement. Jaques-Dalcroze was a music teacher in a conservatory in Vienna. He recognized that students who couldn't feel rhythm also had difficulty learning it through the accepted method of the time (counting). He could see that in those students who were naturally rhythmic, body responses had little to do with intellectual understanding. He began to experiment with movement as a groundwork for perceiving rhythm. His success led him to create more elaborate exercises, which eventually resulted in his being dismissed from the conservatory. He then established his own schools and system, known as Dalcroze Eurythmics.

Finale. Dictionary definition: The concluding part in an entertainment or work, especially a musical composition.

A way of bringing a dance, a class, or a performance to an appropriate finish.

First Position. A ballet term designating a specific placement for arms and feet. This book presents a modified *first position* for the feet. The heels are touching each other; the toes of both feet point away from each other, separated at about a forty-five-degree angle; the knees, whether straight or bent, are aligned over the middle toes.

Forte. An Italian word meaning strong or powerful. Italian is used for most musical terminology. In this book, the word is used to describe the extreme physical energy it would take to create a strong and forceful sound.

Gallop. Dictionary definition: Natural three-beat gait of a horse, faster than a canter, slower than a run.

A basic movement progression in which one foot leaves the ground slightly before the other. For a split second, both feet are off the ground simultaneously, the knees lifted and bent. The first foot returns to the ground slightly before the second foot.

Gluteus Maximus. Dictionary definition: Any of the three large muscles of the buttocks.

Half Time. Making a basic beat half as fast as usual (as used in music and dance). The use of *half time* can be valuable in learning a difficult body technique. In skipping, when the music normally would allow for two skips to take place, the child can step on *one* and hop on *two*, completing one full skip instead of two. In this way, the child can be moving in perfect rhythm, yet have more time for concentration.

Hop. A spring into the air off one foot, followed by landing on the same foot. The entire body is suspended in mid-air for a split second. Hops should be practiced so that each foot is given equal time.

Improvisation. Dictionary definition of *improvise*: To invent, or recite without preparation; to make or provide from available materials.

To move spontaneously, in response to music or rhythm, an emotion, a story, an image, or just the joy of moving. Improvised movement contains a thera-peutic element because it is unself-conscious, unplanned, uninhibited by prejudgment. It is a vehicle for the release of emotions that cannot be expressed verbally.

Compared with a choreographed composition, an improvisation is not set into patterns or rhythms that can be learned and repeated. It remains open to change.

Initiator. The person who creates, originates, or begins the movement. The term is used in preference to the word *leader* in order to bypass the connotation of superiority.

Isolate. Dictionary definition: To separate from a group or whole and set apart.

To move only one specific part of the body. The challenge in doing an isolation movement is to become aware of the joints and muscles necessary to activate only that body part; to become aware of the necessity to control compensatory activity by the rest of the body.

Jump. Dictionary definition: To spring off the ground or other base by a muscular effort of legs or feet.

A jump—as opposed to a hop or a leap —springs off *both* feet and lands on *both* feet. The legs may assume any of a variety of positions.

Laterality. The awareness of the sides of the body. This awareness can best be achieved through movements which focus on activity by each side of the body into space that extends from the center of the body outward.

Leadership. Dictionary definition: The capacity to be a leader; ability to lead.

The genuine confidence that comes with knowing what's expected, an awareness of the needs of others, and a strong sense of responsibility to share one's abilities.

Leap. A spring into the air off *one* foot, involving a transfer of weight in the air followed by landing on the *other* foot. Or a spring into the air off *both* feet, landing on *one* foot. Leaps can be done in any direction, with the body assuming a variety of positions in the air. As opposed to a hop or a jump, a leap *must involve a transfer of weight in the air.*

Legato. Dictionary definition: In an even, smooth style.

A musical term meaning flowing smoothly with no interruption of sound or movement. *Legato* is the opposite of *staccato.*

Ligament. Dictionary definition: A sheet or band of tough, fibrous tissue, connecting two or more bones or areas of cartilage, or supporting an organ or muscle.

Ligaments and muscles need to constantly, carefully, and consistently be worked in order to maintain their elasticity and strength. Ligaments that are torn tend to heal themselves with time, rest, and wet-heat treatments. (See "Warm-Ups," page 33.)

Longitudinal Arch. The arch that extends along the length of the foot.

Lordosis. Dictionary definition: An abnormal forward curvature of the spine in the lumbar region.

Muscle. Dictionary definition: A tissue composed of fiber, capable of contracting and relaxing to effect movement.

Muscles can be overdeveloped through constant contraction. Stretching and extending the muscle counteracts this condition. Children who spend too much time pointing and standing on their toes without balancing this activity with movements like the plié are in danger of developing bulging calf muscles.

Musical Terms. Musical terms are of Italian origin. Although they appear to describe a musical tempo or sound quality, they in fact describe the *movements* that must be made in order to produce these qualities. For instance, the only way a violinist can produce a *legato* sound is to flowingly and smoothly draw the bow across the strings.

Offstage. A theatrical term designating an area accessible from the stage but not visible to the audience.

Pantomime. Dictionary definition: A genre of theatrical performance devised in Rome during the reign of Augustus, in which an actor played all the parts in dumb show, with music and singing in the background. Also called *mime.*

Parallel. Dictionary definition: Being an equal distance apart at every point. *Geometry*: designating two or more straight lines that do not intersect.

Pelvis. Dictionary definition: *Anatomy*: a basin-shaped skeletal structure composed of the innominate bones on the sides, the pubis in front, and the sacrum and coccyx behind, that rests on the lower limbs and supports the spinal column. (The innominate bones are the hip bones. The coccyx is the tail bone.)

Percussion Instruments. Percussion instruments are musical instruments which are struck rather than bowed, plucked, or blown, such as the drums, piano, and xylophone.

Peripheral Vision. Dictionary definition of *peripheral*: The region or area immediately beyond a precise boundary.

The total region that can be seen without moving the head or eyes.

Pizzicato. A musical term indicating music played by plucking rather than by bowing the strings of an instrument. See "Musical Terms."*

Plié. Dictionary definition: A ballet term from the French verb *plier,* meaning *to bend.*

In dance the word is used for a bending of the knees with the feet on the floor. Pliés can be done on one or both feet, in a variety of positions. For a proper plié, an imaginary plumb line dropping from the knee should land over the middle toe, and the body must be properly aligned.

In "Marionettes" (page 42) a *demi-plié* is used. *Demi* means half. This describes a plié in which the heels remain on the ground while the body is only partially lowered. For a *grand plié* the dancer would go as low as possible, depending on the body position.

Radius. Dictionary definition: A line segment that joins the center of a circle with any point on its circumference.

Relaxation. Dictionary definition: The act of relieving tension and strain.

All movement requires that some muscles become tense while others relax. One of the goals in learning body techniques is to become aware of which body parts require tension and which must remain relaxed to achieve a given movement.

Rhythm. Dictionary definition: Any kind of movement characterized by the regular recurrence of strong and weak elements.

Rhythm denotes the regular, patterned flow, the ebb and rise of sounds or movement in speech, music, writing, dance, and natural phenomena.

Scootch. An expression coined by the author, meaning to shuffle with tiny steps, feet flat on the ground and knees bent.

Second Position. A ballet term meaning that the feet are separated laterally.

Spotting. A ballet term meaning turning the head in such a manner as to see nothing but a chosen point of focus.

How to spot: look at a point of focus while turning your body, until that point can no longer be seen. Then (keeping the body still) turn your head sharply and once again focus on the same point. The sharp movement of the head brings the body to a completion of the turn.

Staccato. A musical term meaning disconnected, abrupt, crisp, sharp, and cut-off. The opposite of *legato*. See "Musical Terms."*

Sternum. The breastbone.

Stretch. See "Extend."*

Surface. Dictionary definition: The outer or the topmost boundary of an object.

Sway. To move rhythmically back and forth or side to side in a kind of gentle swinging motion. A sway produces the internal image of a huge pendulum. The body weight drops with gravity and recovers, drops and recovers, with rhythmic momentum.

Tap. Dictionary definition: To strike gently and audibly.

It is unlikely that a sound will be produced with bare feet against a hard floor, but the tactile sensation of the toe striking a surface creates the necessary kinaesthetic response. See "The Swimming Pool," page 46.

Tempo. Dictionary definition: A musical term meaning the relative speed at which a composition is to be played; pace.

Tempo is different from *rhythm* in that it is concerned with speed, while *rhythm* is concerned with a repeatable pattern of beats. See "Rhythm."*

Tension. Contracting or extending any body parts with extreme energy or force. The opposite of *relaxation.*

Tensions carried within the body over long periods of time can appear to be and feel normal. They can become part of the body structure. Awareness through movement can help correct and change this situation.

Thighs. Dictionary definition: The portion of the human leg between the hip and the knees.

In normal urban living, thigh muscles are rarely developed. They require dance movement or athletic exercise to become strong.

Torso. Dictionary definition: The trunk of the human body.

The torso is used in a variety of ways in different dance forms. In the old traditional ballet technique, it is held fairly static, while most of the active movement takes place in the extremities—the legs, arms, and head.

Isadora Duncan revolutionized dance by proclaiming that emotions stem from and are expressed through the torso. Modern dance has followed the Duncan tradition by making the torso the focal point of body techniques. The movements of the extremities extend out of the movements of the torso.

Tune in. Dictionary definition: To become attuned.

To be able to relax and be open enough to become sensitive and aware of one's own feelings, the feelings of others, and the environment.

Turn-out. A ballet term meaning a position of the legs resulting from rotating the thighs so that the knees and the feet point away from each other. When the feet are forced to open wider than is allowed by the natural opening in the pelvis, the back is thrown out of alignment and lordosis results. See "Body Alignment" (page 83) and "First Position."*

Upbeat. Dictionary definition: An unaccented beat, upon which the conductor's hand is raised; especially, the last beat of a measure.

Upstage. Dictionary definition: Pertaining to or involving the rear of a stage.

A theatrical term which stems from the days when stages were tilted and the audience areas were level. Performers standing farthest away from the audience were "up stage." To upstage has come to mean to distract the audience's attention from another performer to oneself.

259

Index to the Movement Activities

Other Barlin Teaching Materials

Books

The Art of Learning Through Movement
Dance-A-Folk-Song
Move and be Moved (with Tamara Greenberg)
Hello Toes!

Records & Cassettes

Dance-A-Story Cassette Series
Cloud Journeys (with Marcia Berman)
Dance-A-Story: Sing-A-Song (with Marcia Berman)
Rainy Day Dances, Rainy Day Songs
  (with Marcia Berman & Patty Zeitlin)

Videos

Learning Through Movement
Teaching Your Wings to Fly

Films

Learning Through Movement
Teaching Your Wings to Fly

Learning Through Movement
2728 N.C.R. 25E
Bellvue, Colorado 80512